Highway History And Back Road Mystery

Nick Russell

Publishing Partners
Gypsy Journal
Boulder City, Nevada

Copyright © 2004 by Publishing Partners
ISBN 0-9712491-4-8

All rights reserved. No portion of this publication may be reproduced, stored in a retrieval system, or transmitted in any form or by any means, including electronic, mechanical, photocopying, recording or otherwise, without the prior written permission of the publisher, except for brief quotations for the purpose of review.

Published by Publishing Partners
Gypsy Journal RV Travel Newspaper
1400 Colorado Street Suite C-16,
Boulder City, Nevada 89005
E-mail Editor@GypsyJournal.net

Printed in the United States of America

This book is dedicated to my father, Frank Lee Russell, Sr., who taught me to love history and books, and to follow my dreams.

Contents

Introduction	Page 1
Elmer McCurdy	Page 3
The outlaw that was more famous dead than alive	
Belle Boyd	Page 5
Girl spy of the Civil War	
Greenbrier Ghost	Page 11
Victim comes back from the grave for justice	
The Man Who Would Be King	Page 17
A tale of greed, polygamy, assassination, and lost treasure	
He Never Smiled Again	Page 23
Wild Man of the Wynoochee	Page 25
The tragic tale of John Tornow	
The Haunted Wagon Train	Page 31
Sheriff Buckshot Lane	Page 35
Who's Buried In Boone's Tomb	Page 39
Pirate Or Patriot?	Page 43
The Dam Dog	Page 45
Madonna Of The Trail	Page 49
Arizona's Lady Bandit	Page 53
Old Abe	Page 57
Wisconsin's war eagle	
Ohio And Michigan At War	Page 61
Toledo War was a comedy of errors	
William Tell Kidnapped!	Page 65
The Battle Of Picacho Pass	Page 67
A Family Obligation	Page 71
The Mystery Of Lady Bountiful	Page 75
Abe Lincoln Goes To Court	Page 79
Andersonville	Page 81
The South's most notorious prison camp	

America's Stonehenge	Page 87
Rails Over The Water	Page 91
A visit to the S.S. City of Milwaukee	
Christ of the Ohio	Page 99
Little Bighorn Battlefield	Page 101
Historic Cove Fort	Page 105
History Lives At Michilimackinac	Page 109
Dade Battlefield	Page 115
Ethan Allen	Page 119
Vermont's Revolutionary War hero	
Fort Caroline	Page 123
European foothold in the New World	
Pioneer Grave	Page 127
Fort Meigs	Page 131
Bastion of the War of 1812	
A Stolen Shrine	Page 135
George Washington Carver	Page 139
From slave to scientist	
The Long Walk	Page 143
The tragedy of the Navajo people	
White Dove of the Desert	Page 147
Old Ironsides	Page 153
America's proudest warship	
The Whitman Tragedy	Page 161
The Ghosts of Yuma Territorial Prison	Page 165
Do convicts still haunt the old cellblocks?	
Yulee Sugar Mill Ruins	Page 171
A look into Florida's past	
The Witches of Salem	Page 175
Georgia's Paul Revere	Page 181
Haunted New Orleans	Page 183

Poker Alice	Page 189
The Mad Bomber of Bath	Page 193
The Pig War	Page 197
Dillinger's Tommy Guns Come Home	Page 199
The Peshtigo Fire	Page 205
Monument to a Camel Jockey	Page 213

Highway History And Back Road Mystery

Introduction

    I have the best job in the world. For several years I have made my living by wandering down America's highways and back roads looking for the forgotten historical site, the oddball museum, and the overlooked treasures that seem to have been pushed aside by the constant search for whatever is newer, bigger, and better.

    I tell the stories of the places I find in the *Gypsy Journal*, the 36-page bi-monthly tabloid newspaper for recreational vehicle owners and armchair travelers that my wife Miss Terry and I publish from the road in our motorhome. Our readers have all been to Disney World and Dollywood, they've been entertained in Branson, and experienced the Grand Canyon. Now they are looking for something a bit slower paced and off the beaten track. I always tell my friends that basically I make my living by telling other people where to go! That's a pretty good gig, when you think about it.

    I am fascinated with history and always enjoy finding the stories behind the stories. Everybody has heard of Paul Revere, the Boston silversmith who rode off into the night to warn patriots that the British were coming. But have you ever heard of John Henry Wisdom, the Paul Revere of the South? His midnight ride was longer than Paul Revere's, and unlike the Boston nightrider, Wisdom rode further and completed his mission. (Paul Revere was actually captured by a British patrol, and two other men went on to spread the word of British troop movements.) Who doesn't know about the great Chicago fire? But did you know that on the very same night that parts of Chicago burned, further north in Wisconsin an entire town was burned to the ground, resulting in far greater loss of life?

    In *Highway History and Backroad Mystery* I want to share with you some of the interesting trivia and history we have discovered in our travels, along with some unanswered questions that I find intriguing. One such case is West Virginia's Greenbriar Ghost. Did a young murder victim really come back from the grave to see justice done? Surely you know the story of frontiersman Daniel Boone, and maybe you have even visited his tomb in the state capitol in Frankfort, Kentucky. But who is really buried there? The answer might surprise you!

We'll explore these and many more stories in this book, all discovered on lonesome backroads or along busy highways where travelers never seem to take the time to stop and look past the neon signs and tourist traps to see the real America. It's still out there, waiting for us to come and rediscover it.

Elmer McCurdy

The outlaw that was more famous dead than alive

Have you ever heard the term "worth more dead than alive"? For one Oklahoma outlaw, the words could have been changed just a bit to "more famous dead than alive." We learned the strange story of his life and death while touring the Oklahoma Territorial Museum in Guthrie.

While Elmer McCurdy didn't amount to much when he was breathing, after he died he became quite a well known person-ality. McCurdy was a smalltime petty thief and bumbler who turned to train robbery, hoping to increase both his take and his reputation. With a gang of equally inept cohorts, McCurdy robbed a passenger train, but the pickings were slim. The outlaws got away with only a passenger's revolver and a few dollars.

Determined to do better the next time, McCurdy and his pals held up another train a few days later, on October 4, 1911. The train was supposed to be carrying over $400,000 in cash. But again the outlaws goofed, robbing the wrong train. Only after blowing out the entire side of the baggage car with a too-heavy charge of nitroglycerine and dynamite, did the robbers realize their error. Their loot from this heist was only $40, a coat, a pocket watch, and two gallons of whiskey. Drowning his sorrows in booze, McCurdy was drunk when a posse caught up with him three days later and killed him. That was when the bizarre odyssey of Elmer McCurdy really began.

The outlaw's body was taken to a funeral home for embalming, but nobody came forward to claim it. So for the next five years, McCurdy's remains stood propped up in a corner of the mortuary, where people frequently used him as a hall tree to hang their hats and coats on.

Finally, sometime in 1916, five years after his death, a man showed up at the Oklahoma mortuary claiming to be a relative of Elmer McCurdy coming to take his remains for a proper burial. But the long lost relative was actually a con man, who put the outlaw on display at carnival sideshows around the country.

For many years McCurdy toured the country as the "Oklahoma Outlaw," the "Dope Fiend," and the "1,000 Year Old Man." Carnival crowds in small towns from border to border viewed the body, coming away thrilled and titillated with their taste of the "wild life." McCurdy even made the big screen, as a prop in the 1950s movie *She Freak*. Sometime after that, the outlaw's body seems to have dropped out of sight.

Years later workers were renovating an old California arcade style fun house for the 1970s television program the *Six Million Dollar Man*, when a crew member accidently knocked the arm off a dummy. When he attempted to repair it with electrical tape, he noticed a bone sticking out. The police and coroner were called, and investigation revealed the "dummy" was in reality our long lost outlaw friend, Elmer McCurdy.

California authorities contacted Oklahoma, and only after it was promised that McCurdy would be given a respectful burial was the body released. On April 22, 1977, outlaw Elmer McCurdy was buried with full honors in Guthrie, Oklahoma's Summit View Cemetery, his long years as a celebrity on the road finally over.

Belle Boyd
Girl spy of the Civil War

    The jet boat rides, roller coasters, miniature golf courses, souvenir shops and other tourist attractions of Wisconsin Dells are a long way from the bloody battlegrounds of the Civil War, but there is a connection between this Midwest fun land where families come to play and that terrible conflict where brothers, fathers, and sons sometimes faced each other over the barrels of their muskets. In a peaceful cemetery just a couple of miles from all of the activity in downtown Wisconsin Dells is the grave of one of the most controversial figures of the War Between the States.

    Born in Martinsburg, Virginia (now West Virginia), on May 9, 1843, Maria Isabella Boyd was the daughter of a prominent and proud southern family. Her father, Ben Boyd, was a wealthy merchant, and the fine Greek Revival home he built in Martinsburg in 1853 still stands today at 123 East Race Street. The family had several children who died at early ages, and by the start of the Civil War, Maria Isabelle, known as Belle, was the oldest child. She attended Mount Washington Female College in Baltimore from 1856 to 1860, and was formally presented to Washington, DC society just before the war began.

Ben Boyd joined the Virginia Cavalry at the outbreak of hostilities, leaving his wife behind in Martinsburg to care for the teenaged Belle, her younger sister and brother. From the early days of the war, the area around Martinsburg was in the middle of the struggle. When Union soldiers took the area, the independent and headstrong Belle was suddenly thrust into the limelight. On July 4, 1861 a group of Union troopers attempted to raise the Stars and Stripes over the Boyd house. "Our family would rather die first," Mrs. Boyd declared, and a Union soldier struck the woman with his fist. Pulling a hidden pistol from her dress, Belle promptly shot her mother's assailant dead.

The teenager was arrested and charged with murder, but the killing was ruled justifiable homicide. Even though she had taken the life of one of their own, many of the Union officers and soldiers admired Belle's beauty and spunk, as well as her courage in the face of a bully. Remember, these were still days of chivalry, and the dead soldier's actions in attacking Belle's mother were frowned upon by his own comrades.

Belle took advantage of her popularity, mingling with the Union officers and eavesdropping on their conversations. The information she learned was then passed along to Confederate leaders. When one of Belle's missives was intercepted, such was her popularity (and possibly so gullible were the enemy officers), that she only received a stern reprimand.

By now eighteen years old, Belle continued her spying activities, many times relaying vital information to rebel leaders. She was praised during the Battle of Front Royal in May, 1862 for providing rebel forces with information that helped them capture several vital positions. Betrayed by a former lover, Belle was arrested on July 29, 1862. Charged with being a spy, she was held for a month in the Old Capitol Prison in Washington, DC. But again her charms seem to have prevailed, and the southern beauty was released in a prisoner exchange, and went to live with her aunt in Fort Royal, Virginia.

Undaunted by her arrest, Belle continued to gather intelligence for the southern cause. In Fort Royal, she overheard Union General James Shield discussing battle plans, and rode on horseback fifteen miles through enemy lines in the dark of night to deliver the news to the Confederate camp. Belle continued her dangerous activities, at times dashing through enemy positions in the heat of battle to bring important news to rebel forces. It is said that more than once, her skirts were pierced with bullet holes, but she never wavered in her cause.

Dubbed "La Belle Rebelle" by a French war correspondent, Belle's daring was recognized by Confederate General Stonewall Jackson, who bestowed upon her the rank of captain and made her an honorary aide-de-camp on his staff. Belle also served as a courier for Jackson and General Beauregarde, as well as a scout for guerilla Colonel John S. Mosby, the "Gray Ghost." In addition to information, Belle also smuggled medical supplies and weapons to southern forces.

Captured again, in June 1863 in Martinsburg, Belle was held in prison until December 1, 1863, when she was released suffering from typhoid. Soon after, she went to England to recover her health, and also to deliver information from Confederate President Jefferson Davis seeking aid for the southern cause from European leaders.

Setting sail for America toward the end of the war, Belle's blockade runner was captured by Union ships. Calling upon her considerable charms, Belle promptly seduced her captor, Captain Samuel Hardinge, and convinced him to allow her to escape to Canada, from which she returned to England. His misdeed found out, Hardinge was later court-martialed and discharged from the Navy.

He followed Belle to England, where the couple were married in August, 1864.

The marriage was short lived. Hardinge died a year later, and with the war over, Belle began a stage career and published a book about her activities during the war titled *Belle Boyd In Camp and Prison*. She returned to America, eventually remarried, and toured for many years, relating her experiences to packed theaters.

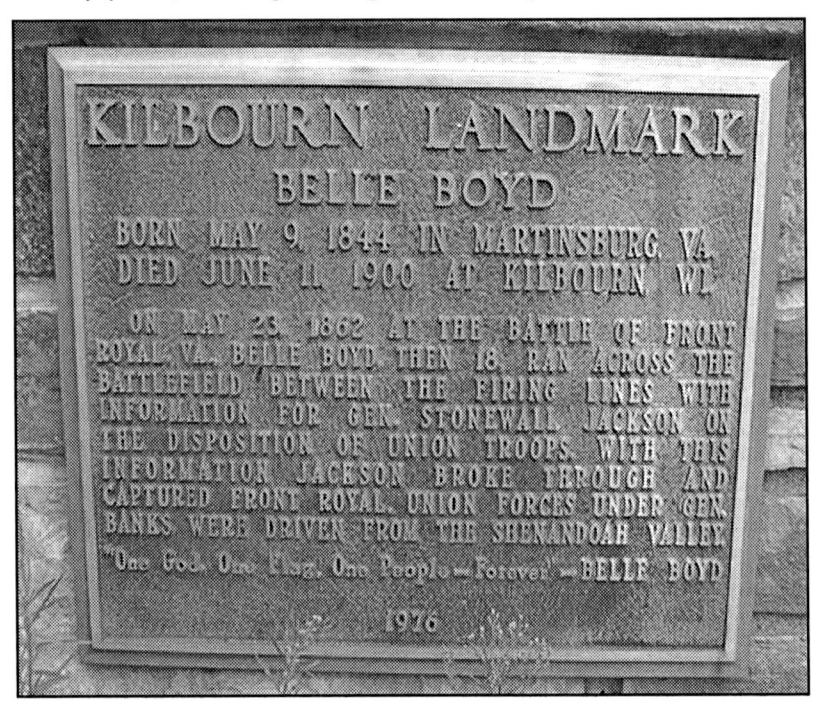

KILBOURN LANDMARK
BELLE BOYD
BORN MAY 9, 1844 IN MARTINSBURG VA.
DIED JUNE 11, 1900 AT KILBOURN WI.

ON MAY 23, 1862 AT THE BATTLE OF FRONT ROYAL VA. BELLE BOYD, THEN 18, RAN ACROSS THE BATTLEFIELD BETWEEN THE FIRING LINES WITH INFORMATION FOR GEN. STONEWALL JACKSON ON THE DISPOSITION OF UNION TROOPS. WITH THIS INFORMATION JACKSON BROKE THROUGH AND CAPTURED FRONT ROYAL. UNION FORCES UNDER GEN. BANKS WERE DRIVEN FROM THE SHENANDOAH VALLEY

"One God, One Flag, One People—Forever"—BELLE BOYD
1976

Belle Boyd died while performing in Kilbourne, Wisconsin on June 11, 1900. But even in death, Belle continued to be the center of controversy. Union veterans were very opposed that a woman they considered a traitor to her country be buried in the same cemetery as northern war dead. They and their descendants were even more offended when a tombstone was placed on Belle's grave that read "*Belle Boyd, Confederate Spy, Born In Virginia, Died In Wisconsin, Erected By A Comrade*" along with a Confederate flag. Strong letters of protest were filed with the Wisconsin governor's office from veteran's groups.

In 1953 a move was made by the United Daughters of the Confederacy to move Belle Boyd's remains for reburial in Virginia, but her daughter resisted, and the former spy still rests in northern soil. Or does she?

There are those who swear that on some moonlight nights the ghostly figure of a young woman riding a horse at a fast pace can be seen on the old battlefields of Virginia's Shenandoah Valley. Could it be the ghost of Belle Boyd, dodging enemy musket balls to deliver messages to a phantom army, still carrying on the cause that she believed in so much?

Highway History And Back Road Mystery

Greenbrier Ghost

Victim Comes Back From The Grave For Justice

Just off Interstate 64 at Sam Black Church, near Lewisburg, West Virginia stands a historical marker to one of the most bizarre mysteries we have ever encountered, the story of a woman's ghost who came back from the grave to see her murderer punished. According to the marker, as well as information on file at the Greenbrier County Historical Society in Lewisburg, it is the only known legal case on record in which the testimony of a ghost helped bring about a conviction.

The strange tale of Zona Heaster Shue began with her birth in 1876. Not much is known of her early years, except that she gave birth to an illegitimate child in 1895. A year later, in October 1896, she met and married Erasmus (Edward) Stribbling Trout Shue, a handsome stranger who arrived in

Greenbrier County and found work as a blacksmith.

Most reports say that Edward Shue was a likable enough fellow, though Zona's mother took an immediate dislike to her new son-in-law. She felt that beneath his outgoing facade there lurked dark secrets. Later revelations would prove her suspicions were right. Zona's family tried to stand in the way of her budding romance to the older man, but Shue managed to convince the fifteen year old girl to marry him while she was visiting her uncle on Droop Mountain.

The newlyweds set up housekeeping in a two-story frame house in Livesay's Mill, but their time together would be short. Just two months after the wedding, on January 23, 1897, Shue sent a young boy named Anderson Jones to his home to do some chores for Zona. When no one answered his knock on the door, young Anderson went inside and discovered the body of Zona on the floor, her lifeless eyes staring at the ceiling. The boy would later testify that Zona appeared peaceful, though the position of her body was strange for someone who might have collapsed suddenly. She was lying on her back, her feet together, one arm to her side, the other stretched across her abdomen. The terrified boy ran to Shue's blacksmith shop and told him of his gruesome discovery.

A local doctor named George Knapp was summoned, but it took him nearly an hour to arrive over primitive mountain trails. What the doctor found upon his arrival at the Shue house was a peculiar sight. Though seemingly devastated at the loss of his bride, Edward Shue had taken the time to carry his wife's body upstairs to their bedroom, where he dressed her in her best dress, a high-collared garment, and tied a veil over her face and tied it in a large bow under her chin. The bereaved husband sat cradling Zona's head in his arms and sobbing, and when the doctor attempted to examine the body, Shue reacted so violently that the doctor left, but not before noticing some strange bruising on Zona's neck.

Whatever he may have thought of the bruises or Edward Shue's strange behavior, Doctor Knapp first listed her cause of death as heart failure, and later changed the cause to "childbirth," though there was no evidence that Zona was pregnant. The doctor did state that the young bride had been treated two weeks prior to her death for "female trouble."

Zona's body was laid out for viewing in the couple's living room, and during her wake, friends and relatives observed several things. Edward had tied a large scarf around Zona's neck, and cradled her head with pillows on both sides. He never left Zona's side, and discouraged anybody who attempted to get too close to the body. But more than one grieving visitor noticed a strange looseness to Zona's head. Still, Zona Shue was buried in the small cemetery of Soule Chapel Church, a few miles from Rainelle. But the tragic story was far from over.

People were talking about Edward Shue's strange behavior following the death of his wife, and Zona's mother, Mary Jane, was convinced there was more to her daughter's death than had been revealed. Mary Jane told people that she lay in her bed night after night praying that the truth about Zona's death would be revealed. Apparently, her prayers were answered.

Four weeks after Zona's death, her mother reported that she had appeared at her bedside. The first night, Zona only looked sadly at her mother before disappearing. Was it a dream? Mary Jane insisted that she had been wide awake, praying when Zona came to her.

The apparition came again the next night, and then for two more nights in a row. Mary Jane reported that Zona had told her that Edward Shue had been a violent man, and had flown into a rage the night before her body was discovered, because dinner had not been waiting on the table when he arrived home from work. Zona reported that after screaming at her and pushing her, Edward Shue had grabbed her by the neck and violently twisted it, killing her instantly.

When Mary Jane revealed the information she had been told by Zona's ghost, many neighbors at first thought they were only hearing the ramblings of a grief-stricken mother, while others thought she might have been dreaming. Mary Jane insisted she had been wide awake on all four visits, and began to describe Zona's home and other spots around Livesay's Mill, which she had never seen. People began to think that there might be more to Mary Jane's story than they first

Highway History And Back Road Mystery

believed.

Mary Jane was able to convince the prosecuting attorney in Lewisburg that the death needed further investigation, and Zona's body was exhumed. An autopsy revealed that Zona had indeed died of a broken neck and crushed larynx!

Edward Shue was arrested and held for trial in Lewisburg. Soon dark details from his past began to emerge. In 1886 Shue and his first wife had lived in Pocahontas County, West Virginia. Shue had reportedly beaten his wife on a regular basis, until she finally divorced him while he was in prison serving a term for horse theft. It didn't take Shue long to remarry, this time to another young woman, who died under mysterious circumstances. Shue reported that the woman had been killed when she tripped and struck her head on a rock, though there had been no other witnesses to the accident, and Edward Shue had insisted the body be buried without an examination.

Perhaps because he may have gotten away with murder once before, Shue was confident he would this time too. He boasted to friends from jail that "they cannot prove I did it!" He was in for a letdown when his trial began in Lewisburg on June 30, 1897. Edward Shue's defense attorney tried to discredit Mary Jane's testimony about her ghostly visitations, trying to make her admit that they were mere dreams. But Mary Jane would not be swayed. She insisted from the witness stand that she had been wide awake and that Zona's visits were indeed very real. A jury apparently felt Mary Jane made a credible witness, because Edward Shue was convicted of murder and sentenced to life in prison.

Local residents, enraged by the murder, attempted to take the matter into their own hands, and a lynching was attempted, but lawmen snuck Shue out of town before the mob could get to him. Shue was lodged in the Moundsville Penitentiary, where he died a few years after his trial.

Skeptics may doubt the claim that Zona Shue's ghost really came back from the grave to reveal the truth about her death, but old newspapers in the Historical Society in Lewisburg report the story of

Highway History And Back Road Mystery

Edward Shue's trial, and according to *Case Comment*, a nationally published attorney's magazine, the case of the murder of Zona Heaster Shue is the only one in the United States where a person was convicted of murder based upon the testimony of a ghost.

The roadside marker about the Greenbrier Ghost is located on US Highway 60, just a few feet south of Exit 156 off Interstate 64. Zona Shue's grave is in the cemetery of the Soule Chapel Church, which is located on Farmdale Road, about 1/4 mile off the James River and Kanawa Turnpike (Old Highway 60), approximately seven miles south of Rainelle, West Virginia. Despite the impressive name, the old turnpike is a very narrow mountain road, and not suitable for large vehicles. Zona's gravestone reads "In Memory of Zona Heaster Shue, Greenbrier Ghost 1876-1897." If you are visiting the hills of West Virginia, take the time to stop by and pay your respects to the Greenbrier Ghost.

Highway History And Back Road Mystery

The Man Who Would Be King

Greed, polygamy, assassination, and lost treasure

Did you know that long after the American Revolution displaced the British king, Michigan had its own self-proclaimed monarch, who ruled with an iron hand for six years?

The story of James Jesse Strang has all of the ingredients of a classic work of fiction, including a political power struggle, a greedy antagonist, sexual intrigue, behind the scenes treachery, murder, and the mystery of a fortune in gold never recovered. But all of this really took place in nineteenth century Michigan, not in the pages of a novel. As in many cases, truth can be stranger than fiction.

Born in New York in 1813, Strang studied law and was admitted to the Bar. He worked as an attorney, served as a Baptist minister, and became the postmaster of Chatauqua, New York at a young age. The government appointment didn't last long, and when he lost his position as postmaster, Strang, by now with a wife and three children, moved to Wisconsin in 1843.

A year later Strang met Joseph Smith, founder of the Mormon church, in Nauvoo, Illinois, and quickly became a convert. It didn't take long for the ambitious young man to become appointed an elder in the church.

Shortly after Strang joined the faith, Mormon leader Smith was assassinated while in jail, awaiting trial for destroying a newspaper office. Strang immediately claimed succession, telling church members that Smith had told him he was to become the next leader of the faith. Brigham Young contested Strang's claim, and following a heated battle for the title, was appointed the leader of the Mormon Church. Young quickly excommunicated Strang, and shortly thereafter led his people to Utah.

Strang and his handful of dissident followers then went to Voree, Wisconsin, at present-day Spring Prairie. Strang claimed to have found mysterious ancient brass tablets that bore strange symbols, including a man holding a scepter and wearing a crown, surrounded by stars. He told his followers he had been visited by an angel, who told him the tablets were proof of Strang's destiny as a leader of his people.

Strang quickly proved himself to be a stern taskmaster, strictly regulating every aspect of life for his followers. Materialism was denounced, sexual morality was strict, since Strang did not believe in polygamy, and eating meat was forbidden. His followers seemed to accept Strang's rules, and all went well for a time, until an increase in non-Mormons in the area began to concern the church leader. Believing these outsiders would disrupt his congregation's lifestyle, Strang moved his people to Beaver Island, located in Lake Michigan off the coast of Michigan, due west of Cross Village.

On July 8, 1850, Strang declared himself king of his followers and the island, and began demanding tithes not only of his followers, but from all of Beaver Island's residents and the fishermen who worked the waters around the island. Those who refused to pay were rumored to have been whipped or mysteriously disappeared. Strang even ordered the county treasurer to pay him one-tenth of all taxes collected on the island.

The gentiles on Beaver Island bitterly opposed Strang's rise to power and his demands, but they couldn't long withstand the force of "King" Strang and his dedicated followers. Those who did not belong to Strang's band were forced off the island in fear for their lives. Local lore says that more than one island farmer who stood up to King Strang met with an unfortunate accident or saw his barn burned down.

With the gentiles gone, Strang's reign on Beaver Island became absolute, and he imposed even stricter rules and demands on his people. He erected a huge log temple, made church attendance compulsory, built a sawmill, established schools, and founded his own newspaper, the *Northern Islander*, demanding even larger tithes to pay for his projects. Strang also used his printing press to publish books and pamphlets proclaiming his divine guidance and defending his reign.

Understandably, there was tremendous tension and resentment between the local people and Strang's band. Not content to rule just Beaver Island, Strang tried to spread his sphere of power in a wider circle, onto the mainland. Strang disapproved of liquor, and worked to stop local whiskey trade, as well as interfering with fur trading and other long established commercial ventures. Blood was spilled more than once as long time residents clashed with the Mormons under Strang.

Long an opponent of polygamy, that all changed when Strang took a second wife, Elvira Field, a former school teacher. Before the marriage, Field had disguised herself as a man and traveled with Strang under the name of Charles Douglas, claiming to be his assistant. Strang's first wife, unhappy with his conversion to polygamy, fled the island with their children and returned to Wisconsin. Undeterred, in 1852 Strang took a third wife, and two more in 1855, eventually fathering twelve children by his five wives. Strang declared that by his divine imperative, the elders in his church must also become polygamists and each must have at least two wives. The idea was not widely embraced on Beaver Island, and only a handful of Strang's followers, not more than twenty, took a second wife.

As time went on, Strang's power-mad demands on his people became even more bizarre. He dictated what they would eat, who they would marry, and how they would dress. Strang banned long skirts on women, and demanded that they wear bloomers made in a calico print. He was rumored to demand physical favors from the island's women, married or unmarried, as was his right as monarch.

July 8 was declared King's Day on Beaver Island, and the day was a celebration of King Strang. Festivities included burnt offerings, the paying of tributes to the king in the form of livestock and fowl, and feasting and dancing.

Highway History And Back Road Mystery

Beaver Island and its neighboring islands were connected to Mackinac Island for judicial and electric purposes, and by 1851 Strang and his followers controlled all of the political offices on Mackinac Island. Typical of many politicians, Michigan's governor and legislature chose to overlook Strang's bizarre hold on Beaver Island in favor of cultivating the votes of his congregation.

However, the unrest caused by Strang in the surrounding area did not go unnoticed. Eastern newspapers denounced his iron rule, and sentiment against Strang and his group reached Washington. In 1851 President Millard Fillmore ordered the naval warship *Michigan* to transport a U.S. Marshall and his deputies to Beaver Island to arrest Strang and his leadership cadre. They were lured aboard the ship on a ruse and taken into custody without bloodshed. Charged with federal offenses including interfering with the U.S. mail, counterfeiting, unlawful taxation, and cutting timber on public lands, Strang and nearly 100 of his faithful were taken to Detroit, where they stood trial.

What came next was a shock to Strang's opposition. Calling on his former legal skills as an attorney in New York, the "King" conducted his own defense and won! His political power further strengthened by his victory, Strang led his group back to Beaver Island, much to the dismay of local residents. If they thought King Strang was a thorn in their side before, they were in for a rude awakening. Strang used the influence of his flock's votes to get himself elected to two terms in the State Legislature.

Tensions were just as high among some of the Mormons on Beaver Island as they were on the mainland. Strang was a strong believer in corporal punishment, and administered public whippings for everything from dress code violations to not showing him the proper respect. When one of Strang's followers, Thomas Bedford, was accused of having an affair with the wife of his business partner, Strang ordered the sinner to be punished with 79 lashes.

The humiliated Bedford associated himself with disillusioned Mormons from Strang's followers, unhappy fishermen, and

Mackinac Island residents and began to plot revenge. On June 16, 1856 Bedford led an ambush against Strang, and the King of Beaver Island was felled by a barrage of gunfire. Surviving the attack, but mortally wounded, Strang was transported to Voree, Wisconsin, where it is said he died in his first wife's arms on King's Day, July 8, 1856. Shortly thereafter, a mob of drunken Mackinac Islanders and fishermen descended on Beaver Island and attacked the Mormons in a rage of burning and looting. Those who survived the attack fled the island and scattered.

    The King may be gone from Beaver Island, but his legacy remains today. Legend has it that Strang amassed a fortune in gold during his reign, and hid it somewhere near Fox Lake on the island. Treasure hunters have searched for the loot but no one has ever reported finding it. Does it still lie hidden somewhere on Beaver Island today?

Highway History And Back Road Mystery

He Never Smiled Again

There are many interesting tales of tragedy and heroism associated with Great Lakes shipwrecks, and one we found intriguing was that of the steamship *Independence*, and one of her crewmen, Amos Stiles, the man who never smiled again.

The *Independence* was built in Chicago in 1844, and her owner, J. M. Averill originally intended her to be used in the trans-Atlantic trade. The wooden hulled ship was 119 feet long, with a width of 26 feet. Averill's dreams of financial success with his ship quickly turned into a nightmare when it was determined the *Independence* could not carry enough fuel to travel such a great distance. Another setback was the discovery that the ship's Ericson propeller had design flaws that made it so agonizingly slow that a man walking could travel faster than *Independence* could at full power.

Realizing his new ship's limitations, Averill had her outfitted with sails to increase her speed, and *Independence* was modified and put into service on the expanding Great Lakes shipping routes. Portaged around the rapids at Sault Ste. Marie, Michigan in a slow overland journey taking seven weeks, *Independence* was launched in Lake Superior, becoming the first steamship to sail the lake's treacherous waters.

The shipping industry on Lake Superior is a dangerous business, and was even more so in the early days before radar, radio communications, and satellite-aided navigation. Any number of dangers awaited the men who sailed the lake's hazardous waters, from the perils of hidden shoals and reefs, to collisions with other vessels, fires, and the constant threat of bad weather. *Independence* would prove to be yet another victim of the lake's dangers.

On April 21, 1853 the ill-fated ship met her end in a sudden and violent manner. *Independence* left Sault Ste. Marie heavily loaded with winter supplies destined for settlements on Lake Superior's western shore. Soon after she left port, a boiler exploded and the little steamer plunged to the bottom, taking four of her crew with her to watery graves. *Independence*, the first steamship to sail Lake Superior, became the first steamship to perish on the lake.

One crewman from the *Independence*, Amos Stiles, survived the explosion when he was blown skyward and landed in the frigid water. Struggling to stay afloat, Stiles managed to grab a bale of hay that was floating among the wreck's debris, and used it as a life raft.

The brave sailor was not safe yet. Superior had more trials to test his will to live. The current swept Stiles a half mile through churning rapids, where he bounced over rocks and fought to keep his head above water. Having escaped death twice within a very short time, Stiles was eventually pulled from the water and saved.

Some say it was nerve damage suffered from his traumatic experience, while others claim it was the terrible memories he carried from the wreck, when he saw his shipmates go under, and narrowly escaped death himself, but for whatever reason, Amos Stiles wore a permanent frown from that day onward, and became known in Lake Superior lore as The Man Who Never Smiled Again.

Highway History And Back Road Mystery

Wild Man of the Wynoochee
The tragic tale of John Tornow

Washington state's Olympic Peninsula is wild country even today, thousands of square miles of dense rainforest, broken here and there by deep rivers and steep hills to the south, giving way to towering mountains in the north. Even today, in this age of high speed transportation and satellite communications, the Olympic Peninsula forces man to slow down and live at her pace. Nearly 100 years ago the forests of the Peninsula were even wilder, and the men and women who lived in these forbidding woods had to be a match for the unforgiving land they inhabited. It was uncivilized territory in many ways, where people had to rely on their own means to survive, and often those means were cruel. In this untamed land, filled with rough, hard working men, one man's name stood out from all the others. A name that could strike fear into the hearts of the boldest loggers and trappers. That man was John Tornow.

Popular belief has it that John Tornow was a deranged killer, a wild man who roamed the Wynoochee River country, preying on loggers and timber cruisers, murdering them for their clothing and what meager property they might be carrying with them. For nearly two years armed posses launched futile searches for Tornow, always one step behind the fugitive. The dramatic end to the chase came on April 16, 1913, when Tornow was cornered and killed in a shootout at his camp deep in the woods. But was John Tornow really the monster popular history has labeled him? Or was he simply a tragic figure, caught up in circumstances he could not control and reacting in the only way he knew?

Over the years, many stories have been told about Tornow. As with most legends, the fiction outweighs the facts, as each storyteller embellished the tale and it was passed from campfire to logging camp to barroom. But the true facts have never fully come to light. The mysterious story of John Tornow is one whose whole truth will probably never be known.

What *is* known is that Tornow was born September 4, 1880. His German immigrant parents settled on the Olympic Peninsula at Matlock, west of Shelton, and carved a homestead out of the forest. Life on the frontier was harsh under the best of circumstances, and the humble Tornow holdings were modest. John Tornow wasn't cut out for life as a farmer, and was happiest roaming the forests alone. An excellent shot, his hunting prowess kept the family table in game to supplement the meager diet the farm offered at times.

Apparently Tornow was considered somewhat of an oddball by some people in the small community, and he was committed to an insane asylum in Olympia at one time. Was this due to any aberration on his part? Perhaps not - some believe the commitment was a move to declare Tornow unfit to claim his inheritance from the deaths of his parents, possibly instigated by his brother-in-law, Henry Bauer. To Tornow, life in the asylum was life in prison, and he promptly ran away and back to the security of his woods.

The next act in the grim story happened in September 1911, and again, more fiction surrounds the incident than fact. Tornow's twin nephews, nineteen year old William and John Bauer, were hunting a bear when they were murdered. Some say their killing may have been related to a cow owned by their parents, Henry and Minnie Bauer. One story has it that John Tornow butchered the cow for meat, and that he murdered the boys to cover up the crime. Others believe that the recluse didn't recognize the youths, seeing only men with guns, and thinking they were a posse come to take him back to the asylum, he ambushed them. The truth is, no one saw Tornow shoot his nephews, and the only evidence linking him to the crime was the discovery of his campsite in the vicinity of the murders.

Whatever happened that terrible day, it was the beginning of the Tornow legend. Perhaps guilty, perhaps innocent but realizing he would be accused of the crime, Tornow fled deeper into the forest. Living off the land, he managed to elude lawmen for nineteen months. As the story circulated around the mining camps and settlements on the lower half of the Olympic Peninsula, John Tornow took on mythical proportions. In the telling, he became a frightening specter, living high in the treetops, swooping down to murder unwary loggers, stripping their bodies of their clothing and supplies and disappearing in the green mists of the forest. The fact that no bodies of murdered loggers were ever found, and that no one actually saw Tornow committing any crime, didn't matter. Never let truth get in the way of a good tale. Yes, men did disappear from time to time in the wild land. It's probable that most of them simply went elsewhere in search of whatever lures men to such untamed territory. Perhaps some did perish in the wilderness. But did they fall victim to a homicidal maniac, or, as is more likely, did they meet up with wild animals or accidents that were all too common in such a rough environment? It didn't matter - John Tornow became the Wild Man of the Wynoochee, and his fate was cast.

Some said Tornow lived on an island in the middle of a small lake, deep in the heart of the forest. They claimed he eluded capture by tethering frogs with string to nearby logs, and when lawmen approached, the frogs' sudden silence served as an alarm system. No one thought to reason that frogs were a natural part of the environment and didn't need to tethered. Or that an experienced woodsman would naturally be attuned to the sounds of the forest and rely on them to warn him of impending danger. Again, the fiction outweighs the facts by a large margin.

On a Spring day in 1913, the searchers finally caught up with the fugitive, and in a wild gun battle, one posse member and John Tornow were killed. The outlaw's body was carried out of the woods and propped up on a board for display, as was the custom in those days. In some saloons and stores on the Olympic Peninsula, they still display photos of the dead fugitive today, a grim reminder of the country's frontier past.

Did John Tornow kill his nephews, precipitating the manhunt? There is reason to believe not. Tornow loved his sister, Minnie, and doted on her twin boys. There may have been others who had reason to commit the crime. Their father, Henry Bauer, disappeared from the area shortly after the murders, never to be seen again. Some speculate that he may have been the true killer, and that John Tornow was framed, either to cover up the killer's identity or to cheat him out of his share of the family homestead.

Yes, Tornow killed a lawman when they closed in on his camp, but was this the act of an outlaw, or the desperate reaction of a disturbed soul fearing a return to a confinement it could not survive? Was John Tornow a cold blooded killer, or simply an outcast caught up in a terrible tragedy he did not create and could only react to? No one will ever know. All of the principals are dead now, and the mystery remains.

John Tornow is buried in the tiny Grove Cemetery, near Matlock. Nearby are the graves of his nephews, William and John Bauer, and their sister Mary, as well as Tornow's parents. John Tornow's headstone depicts his nephews on their bear hunt, and describes Tornow as follows: "From Loner - To Outcast - To Fugitve." Perhaps one final insult to an unfortunate life is that the

Highway History And Back Road Mystery

word fugitive is misspelled on the headstone. Or perhaps John Tornow wouldn't care - he's finally at peace in his beloved wilderness.

Highway History And Back Road Mystery

The Haunted Wagon Train

Just east of Raymond, Washington, on Highway 6, a historical marker sits near the grave of Willie Keil. Over the years, untold numbers of travelers have stopped to read the sign, but not many of them know the story behind the marker - the story of the dead man who led a wagon train of settlers through Indian Territory along the Oregon Trail, to the coast of what would one day become Washington state.

In 1855, Willie Keil was a 19 year old man, the oldest son of William Keil Sr., a leader of a group of German Rappites and one of the founders of Bethel, Missouri, where they settled in 1844. The Rappites were a religious sect named after their founder, George Rapp, who lived a communal lifestyle where everyone worked for the good of the colony. Keil's colony of Rappites, about 200 strong, broke away from the main sect, moving west. They prospered in Missouri, building sawmills, shops, gristmills, and a distillery where they brewed their own brand of liquor, Golden Rule Whiskey. The Bethel colony lived very well, selling what goods they could not consume themselves to outsiders, including cloth, shoes, and whiskey. Within the colony, no money ever changed hands - everyone took what they needed for their families with no questions asked and apparently no one taking advantage of the system.

After about eleven years, the Bethel, Missouri area became too crowded for the colony and William Keil Sr. sent an advance party of nine men west to scout the frontier for a new site for the commune. The scouts returned in the Spring of 1855, having discovered land in the Willapa Valley, where they cleared some land and began building cabins.

As plans progressed for the move west, young Willie Keil was selected to lead the wagon train, quite an honor for one so young.

But tragedy struck, and Willie died after a short illness. His father was grief-stricken, but he remembered how much his son had wanted to lead the wagon train. William Keil Sr. ordered a special lead lined casket made, where Willie's body was lain. Then the casket was filled with Golden Rule Whiskey and sealed. The wagon containing Willie's remains led the wagon train as they headed west, the emigrants following along behind saying prayers and singing hymns.

Tension between Whites and Indians were high in 1855 as more and more settlers crossed the Plains headed west. Wagon trains were attacked, settlers killed, their wagons looted and burned. Neither man, woman, nor child was safe from the Indians' vengeance at the trespassers. Many wagon trains turned back rather than face the dangers along the trail.

But word of the strange wagon train, led by a dead man, preceded the Rappites. The superstitious Indians wouldn't attack the settlers, though a few visited the wagon train to gawk at the casket. The Keil party was one of a very few wagon trains that crossed the Sioux lands unharmed that violent summer.

Finally, after many months on the trail, the settlers reached their destination near Willapa Bay. During the night of December 26, 1855, in a weird candle lit ceremony that still goes without explanation, and many would consider pagan, young Willie Keil was finally laid to rest on a hilltop. His long journey was over.

But not so for the rest of William Keil Sr's. party. Unhappy with the gloomy sky overhead and the long rainy winter along the coast, Keil led them away, finally settling in the Willamette Valley, where they founded the town of Aurora. Just as they had in Missouri, the colony prospered. The elder Keil led the commune until his own death in 1877.

Highway History And Back Road Mystery

Today Willie Keil's grave sits on its lonely hilltop, and occasionally a passerby will stop to read the sign erected at the base of the hill, never knowing the strange story of how this young man, though departed from life, helped lead his people safely to their new lands.

Highway History And Back Road Mystery

Sheriff Buckshot Lane

Tough Texas lawmen are legendary characters who painted the West with broad brushstrokes, their exploits living on long after their mortal souls have departed this earth, and with every retelling their stories seem to get bigger, until the line between fact and fiction becomes obscured. While Texas *has* produced some justifiably famous heroes, sometimes the tales of the lesser-known peacekeepers are just as colorful. One such man was Sheriff Buckshot Lane, of Wharton County, Texas.

Don't let the name get us off to a wrong start. Though it instantly brings to mind images of wild shootouts, the truth of its origin is much tamer. When he was just a lad, his father perched him on a watermelon, and a family member observed that the youngster's eyes "looked a little buckshot." The moniker stuck and a legend was in the making.

As a young man, Buckshot supported himself with a paper route, delivering the day's news to houses throughout the country. But when he fell in love and got married, he decided he needed a better income, so he ran for sheriff. Some old timers claim his campaign slogan was "Vote for me, or get your paper in the mud." Apparently the threat worked, because folks in Wharton County elected Buckshot to office by a huge margin, launching a career of public service that lasted for over twenty years.

Buckshot soon proved the good citizens of Wharton County had made the right choice, and earned a reputation for honesty and treating people fairly. This was back before the word criminologist had ever been coined, so Sheriff Buckshot employed a common sense approach to law enforcement that seemed to work just fine. He always said there was a difference between the repeat offender and the "accidental" criminal who made a "dishonest mistake," and treated the people he had to arrest appropriately.

Apparently those occasional accidental criminals were sometimes less a thorn in Buckshot's side than the local politicians, whom he seemed to have an ongoing conflict with. More often than not, when politics got in the way of a good decision, Sheriff Buckshot took the law into his own hands, so to speak.

One famous incident concerned the Kerntleton Bridge on Highway 59. Back in the 1930s, the bridge had a bad alignment that caused several serious automobile accidents. Buckshot petitioned local and state officials to have the bridge rebuilt properly, but his requests were ignored. The matter came to a head in 1935 when three young local citizens were killed in an accident on the bridge. Soon after, the span burned mysteriously, forcing the state to rebuild a new, safer bridge.

Speculation as to who the arsonist was flew about the county, and the district attorney said he would purchase the finest suit available as a reward for whoever turned in the culprit. Sheriff Lane waited for ten years, until the statute of limitations had run out on the crime, then promptly turned himself in and demanded his new suit.

Dealing with bootleggers, cowboys, and rough fieldhands, Buckshot was involved in quite a few gunfights. After one shootout, he counted 52 bullet holes in his car, and yet another in the hat he was wearing! Buckshot managed to throw some lead back, and his assailant was taken to the hospital where, as Buckshot later told the story, the bad guy "never got over it."

Sheriff Lane started out carrying a surplus World War I German Luger pistol, but after a gun battle in which three bullets went through a suspect without stopping him, the lawman switched over to a Colt .45 automatic, appreciating the stopping power of the big slab-sided handgun.

In those days, there was little formal training for lawmen – they were handed a gun and badge and told to get to work. Buckshot was a man of science, and taught himself the art of fingerprinting suspects.

When he decided the Sheriff's Department needed an airplane, the County Commissioners overruled him. Not to be outdone, he taught himself to fly and launched a fund-raising campaign, asking citizens to donate $1 each, with the slogan "A buck for Buckshot." He promised that everyone who donated would get their name painted on the side of the airplane, and soon raised $6,500 to become one of the country's first flying lawmen.

Decades before John Walsh brought *America's Most Wanted* to the airwaves, Sheriff Buckshot Lane had his very own radio show on radio station KULP in El Campo. The sheriff was at the microphone every morning for a fifteen minute spot, where he was not above warning the local hooligans that he was after them. It was common for Buckshot to say "Now, Jimmy Smith, you know you've got a warrant out for your arrest. Don't make me come looking for you!" More often than not, the wife beaters, bad check artists, and petty thieves heeded the warning and turned themselves in, not wanting to incur the wrath of Buckshot Lane.

Over time tales of the flamboyant lawman from Wharton County got out, and national magazines like *Time*, *Life*, and the *Saturday Evening Post* magazine sent reporters to interview the rural sheriff with the big reputation. Before long Buckshot was in demand as a speaker and between spending his days chasing criminals and his evenings speaking at Rotary dinners and Ladies Club functions across the region, he spent many hours in the air, flying from one duty to another. Eventually he was even given his own column in the *Houston Post*. There is little doubt that, if he had wanted to, Buckshot Lane could have gone on to a career far beyond the boundaries of his little rural Texas county.

Highway History And Back Road Mystery

But Buckshot wasn't interested. He never forgot where he came from, and was never happier than when he was cruising the back roads and the parking lot of the honkytonks on the lookout for troublemakers and keeping the peace for the citizens who trusted the paperboy enough to give him a badge.

Who's Buried In Boone's Tomb?

Frankfort, Kentucky honors frontiersman Daniel Boone with a beautiful tomb marking the final resting place of the legendary explorer and Indian fighter who opened much of the Bluegrass State to settlement, who is buried there alongside his wife, Rebecca. A marker says this is the grave of Daniel Boone. But who is really buried in Boone's tomb? According to tour guides at the Historic Daniel Boone Home in Defiance, Missouri, Boone still rests in a tiny hilltop cemetery nearby.

Daniel Boone left Kentucky a troubled man, deep in debt and uncomfortable with the "crowds" of settlers who had followed him over the Cumberland Gap into the new frontier. Always restless, Boone sought new frontiers to conquer, and found them in present-day Missouri, then a Spanish holding. Spain granted Boone land in exchange for helping open the territory, as well as for his service as a judge locally.

Life on the frontier had made him a resourceful man, and Boone believed in being prepared. He made cherry wood coffins for himself and Rebecca in expectation of the time when they would pass on. Boone kept his coffin stored under his bed in the handsome home they had built in Missouri, while Rebecca's coffin was stored upstairs in the attic.

It was in 1813 that Daniel Boone and Rebecca set off in a wagon to visit the home of their married daughter, about fourteen miles away. Rebecca fell ill and died either on the journey or shortly after reaching their destination. Daniel returned to their home and retrieved Rebecca's coffin, then returned to bury her in a small hilltop cemetery on his daughter's land.

Daniel Boone lived another seven years, passing away peacefully in his bed on September 26, 1820, probably of pneumonia. His body was placed in his cherry wood coffin and transported to the same cemetery to be buried beside Rebecca. But when the grave was dug, a skeleton was discovered. This wasn't all that odd for the times, as slaves were often buried in unmarked graves in family burial plots. The grave was filled in, and Daniel was buried in a new grave at the foot of Rebecca's.

Years later the state of Kentucky wanted to disinter Daniel and Rebecca and move them to Frankfort for burial in an elaborate tomb to honor Boone's explorations of the state. They opened Rebecca's grave, found the cherry wood casket, and moved it, along with the bones buried beside her, which were not in a coffin. Both were placed in the Kentucky tomb. Missourians probably had a quiet chuckle knowing what the folks in Kentucky didn't.

Highway History And Back Road Mystery

Many years went by, and a state senator from Kentucky was touring the Daniel Boone home in Defiance, Missouri and heard the tale of the mixed up graves. Outraged at such blasphemy, he returned home and ordered an investigation. The Kentucky grave was exhumed and forensics tests run on the bones. The results said the body was that of an African-American male well over six feet tall (Boone was shorter). Still, Kentucky insisted that it had Boone's remains. Time passed and another forensics examination was performed, with the same results. But even today Kentucky insists that Daniel Boone is buried in its soil, while the folks back home in Missouri claim they know otherwise.

So where is Daniel Boone really buried? You will find headstones both in Kentucky and Missouri stubbornly claiming his final resting place. You decided for yourself. I like to think that wherever his mortal remains may lie, Daniel Boone's spirit is still out on the trail somewhere, exploring what's over the next hill.

Highway History And Back Road Mystery

Pirate or Patriot?

Southern Louisiana's history is populated by colorful characters - gambler and knife fighter Jim Bowie, soldier and statesman Andrew Jackson, voodoo queen Marie Laveau, to name just a few. Perhaps no one is as well remembered, or misunderstood, as Jean Lafitte. Depending on who you talk to and which tales you choose to believe, Lafitte was everything from a bloodthirsty pirate to a cultured businessman, to a dedicated patriot. Or maybe all three. Perhaps more than anything, he was the ultimate opportunist.

Jean Lafitte's life is veiled in mystery and legend. It is generally believed he was born in southwestern France somewhere around 1780. Along with his older brother Pierre, Jean Lafitte migrated to the West Indies and later the Louisiana Territory as French privateers. Privateers were little more than pirates legitimized by "licenses" known as letters-of-marque, issued by governments granting them the right to legally prey on enemy shipping. More often than not, privateers didn't limit their activities to just enemy shipping, instead capturing any unfortunate vessel they came across.

Most believe the Lafitte brothers appeared in New Orleans as early as 1802. When the city came under American rule in 1803 with the purchase of the Louisiana Territory from France, Jean Lafitte became a businessman, operating a shop on Royal Street, while Pierre continued to captain ships.

Many pirates frequented the wild Gulf Coast, attacking commercial ships and raiding small coastal towns. The Lafitte brothers became agents for the pirates, smuggling their booty ashore for resale. In 1812 they brothers were captured in the act of smuggling stolen goods and jailed. They promptly hired attorneys, then jumped bail.

The brothers' base of operations was on Grand Terre Island. From there, contraband from captured treasure to slaves was smuggled through the swamps south of New Orleans, called Barataria. Over 1,000 smugglers operated in the region, most under the direction of the Lafitte brothers. Known as Baratarians, they were issued letters-of-marque from the city of Cartagena, in present-day Columbia, to prey on English and Spanish ships. The American government refused to recognize these letters-of-marque, and Governor William C.C. Claiborne considered the Lafitte brothers and their Baratarians criminals.

During the War of 1812, Jean Lafitte recognized his opportunity to achieve legitimate status and a pardon from the American government. When General Andrew Jackson met and defeated overwhelming British force at Chalmette in the decisive Battle of New Orleans, part of the victory had to be acknowledged as coming through the efforts of Lafitte's Baratarians, who he threw into the conflict on the American side. The smugglers fought valiantly and proved their mettle in battle. When the roar of the last cannon shot had faded and the smoke cleared away, Jean Lafitte, pirate and smuggler, was acclaimed as a national hero for helping save New Orleans.

Highway History And Back Road Mystery

The Dam Dog

With its massive concrete walls towered over by high cliffs that soar over the spectacular blue waters of Lake Mead, Hoover Dam is both an engineering marvel and a historic landmark. Every year visitors from around the world come to the canyon where man's vision and industry tamed the mighty Colorado River. With so much to see and experience at the dam, it may be easy to overlook a simple plaque near the escalator to the Visitor Center that is dedicated to the memory of a dog. But the story of the black mutt who became the dam's mascot is one that will touch your heartstrings.

Born under one of the Boulder City barracks built to house the army of workers brought in to build the dam, the dog was a cur of undetermined origins and grossly exaggerated proportions. His feet were much too big for his body, and his rough black fur would have defied any comb, if anyone would have chosen to groom him if he would have tolerated it, which is doubtful. The dog's rough nappy fur earned him the name Nigger, certainly not appropriate in our enlightened society, but remember, this was back in the 1930s, when our nation's conscience had yet to mature. He was blessed with high intelligence and a winning personality that endeared him to the rough and tumble dam workers who populated his world.

When he was only a few weeks old, one of the project supervisors took him to the work site, and immediately the dog knew he was at home. The dam became the only home the dog ever knew or wanted.

Every morning of his life, the dog rode to the project with a work crew. Once at the work site, he spent his days inspecting the construction's progress, riding from one work level to another on the skips, open air elevators used to transport men and equipment. Whenever he wanted to board a skip, the dog would bark for the operator to stop, and when he had arrived at the level he wanted, he would bark again to be let off. His favorite pastime was chasing the ringtail cats that populated the canyon and took up residence in the dam's many tunnels.

It is natural for any animal to shy away from any moving, unstable surface. Professional trainers who work with show business animals consider getting them to overcome this natural aversion among their most difficult tasks. But Hoover Dam's mascot never showed any concern as he ran merrily across swinging catwalks suspended hundreds of feet above the river.

Nobody owned the dog, he was a free spirit loved by all who answered to none. If he wasn't finished with his inspection tour when a work shift ended, or if he decided there were ringtail cats that still needed chasing, he would skip the ride back to town on the transport and hitch a ride later on with a vehicle headed back to the barracks. Nobody ever recalled the dog accepting a ride in any vehicle not connected with the dam project, though nobody could understand how he knew the difference.

Since everybody on the project loved the dog, they were all quick to give him handouts of food, and since he had never heard of a canine version of Weight Watchers, he happily accepted. Eventually this unsupervised diet made him sick, and the concerned dam workers decided he needed a more stable diet. The commissary began to prepare a daily lunch for him, and every day when he boarded the transport, the dog happily carried his lunch sack in his mouth. Once at the work site, the crews would place their lunch pails in a specified area until their lunch break. The dog would put his sack with their lunches and go about his business until the signal blew for break. Then he would run back to his sack and wait patiently until somebody opened it and gave him his lunch.

It became common for the workers to stop by the commissary and leave a dollar or two to cover their mascot's feed bill. Eventually the donations grew to a fair sum, and a bank account was opened for the dog. The funds covered the cost of not only his food, but licences, veterinary bills, blankets, and fancy silver collars that he hated and worked hard to paw off whenever one was put on him.

An indication of how much the dog was loved by his hardworking construction friends was the time a new worker kicked their mascot. He was beaten to a bloody pulp, and may well not have survived if he hadn't been rescued by the Chief Ranger, who then escorted the bruised and battered man out of town with a stern warning never to return.

Once construction was completed, the mascot became an institution at Hoover Dam. The rules said "No Dogs Allowed," and he intended to make sure it was followed. More than one lap dog was chased out of its owners arms and back to the safety of their vehicle by the vigilant watchdog. Chagrined dam tour guides were forced to explain that yes, dogs were prohibited, but no, that rule did not apply to the dam's mascot. More than one guide claimed that the dog actually owned Hoover Dam, and that the Bureau of Reclamation just built and supervised if for him.

He lived out his days chasing ringtail cats, leading tours, and greeting visitors, until one hot and terrible day when a truck backed over him as he snoozed in the shade of a tree. They say it was the saddest day in Boulder City history when news of the dog's death reached town. Tough, work hardened construction workers, no strangers to danger or hardship, wept openly as they chiseled the dog's grave out of the hard rock cliff of the canyon.

    Hoover Dam's mascot rests there today, keeping watch over the dam he loved so much in life. The old dog may be gone, but his memory lives on. Old timers say when the wind howls down the canyon, echoing off the sheer rock walls and swirling around Hoover Dam's towers, the sound is not really made by the gale. It's the dam's canine mascot chasing the ghosts of long dead ringtail cats off his dam.

Highway History And Back Road Mystery

Madonna Of The Trail

They stand as silent reminders of the struggle to tame a wild new world. Twelve tributes to courage, persistence, and sacrifice. They commemorate not the explorers who blazed the path, nor the soldiers and Indian fighters who conquered any resistance to the westward march. They are the Madonnas of the Trail, a series of statues honoring the pioneer women who brought civilization to the frontier.

Back in 1909, a group of Missouri women formed a committee to locate and mark the route of the old Santa Fe Trail in Missouri. Their original plan grew into a movement to develop a national highway. Out of the Missouri effort grew a plan to designate a highway as the National Old Trails Road, and an association was formed by the Daughters of the American Revolution in 1911 to mark the route. Judge Harry S. Truman, of Independence, Missouri was named to head the National Old Trails Road Association.

By an act of Congress, the Old Trails Road would combine a series of historic roads stretching from Washington D.C. to Los Angeles, California into one National Memorial Highway. The Old Trails Road would begin by following the path of Braddock's Road, a route surveyed by a young George Washington and cut through the Allegheny Mountains by British soldiers in 1755 during the French and Indian War. Then the route would follow the course of the Columbia Pike and the Great Valley Road, before picking up the Wilderness Road that frontiersman Daniel Boone cut through the Cumberland Gap, and then following Boone's Lick Road, the Santa Fe Trail, and the Old Trail across the West.

The original plan was to place a series of 3,095 mile markers along the Old Trails Road, but when that was determined to be unfeasible, it was decided that a memorial statue would be placed in each of the twelve states the road passed through.

Inspired by an Oregon statue of Sacajawea, the Shoshone Indian woman who guided the Lewis and Clark Expedition, the statues depict a pioneer woman holding a baby while her young son clings to her skirts. From under her sunbonnet she looks out across the wilderness, her face strong yet gentle. It is the face of a survivor, one who has seen much hardship, and yet knows there is more to follow. She would be known as the Madonna of the Trail.

A sculptor named August Leimbach, who had come to St. Louis from his homeland in Germany, was commissioned to create the statues. Such was his vision of what was needed to honor the pioneer women that it took Leimbach only three days to create the original design.

The Madonna statues are of such proportions as to match the heroic characters of the women they represent. Cast from algonite stone, the statues are ten feet high and weigh five tons. The base upon which they stand is six feet high and weighs twelve tons. On the front pedestal of each statue is inscribed "N.S.D.A.R. Memorial To The Pioneer Mothers Of Covered Wagon Days." The back side of each pedestal reads "The National Old Trails Road." Local historical information is inscribed on the opposite sides of each pedestal.

The first Madonna was dedicated in Springfield, Ohio on July 4, 1928, and the next ten followed within weeks. The last statue was placed in Bethesda, Maryland on April 19, 1929. There was much competition within each state for the honor of being home to the Madonna of the Trail, and their dedications were cause for much celebration and festivity.

Today the Madonna of the Trail statues remain as tributes to the strong women who helped bring civilization to America as they mark the path of our ever expanding western border. To stand before them is to realize that while new lands may be conquered by men with guns and swords, it is through the efforts of women, with spinning wheels and cookstoves that the land is tamed.

The Madonna of the Trail statues can be found in Bethesda, Maryland; Washington County, Pennsylvania; Wheeling, West Virginia; Springfield, Ohio; Richmond, Indiana; Vandalia, Illinois; Lexington, Missouri; Council Grove, Kansas; Lamar, Colorado; Albuquerque, New Mexico; Springerville, Arizona; and Upland, California.

Highway History And Back Road Mystery

Arizona's Lady Bandit

The last stagecoach robbery in the United States took place in 1899 in Arizona. The holdup stands out in history not just because it was the last of its kind, but also because it is the only stagecoach robbery on record by a woman bandit!

Pearl Heart was a rebel in a time when women were expected to be subservient and spend their days raising children and keeping the home fires burning. That sort of life never appealed to Pearl, and she quickly took another course.

Born Pearl Taylor to a wealthy family in Ontario, Canada, Pearl attended the finest schools and seemed to be headed for a comfortable life as a businessman's wife. But Pearl never did what was expected of her. She met a gambler named Frederick Hart and quickly fell in love. She ran away from home and the couple headed for the Columbian Exposition in Chicago. Frederick Hart turned out to be an unskilled gambler who couldn't win a hand of poker if he was the only person sitting at the table. Pearl worked odd jobs to support them, while Frederick lost whatever she earned in card games.

Enthralled with the Wild West shows playing at the Exposition, Pearl became infatuated with the myths and legends of the Old West. She left Frederick just as quickly as she had left her family, and headed for Colorado. No sooner did she arrive than she realized she was pregnant and returned to her family in Canada. By now she was calling herself Pearl Heart, a takeoff on Frederick Hart's name, though it is uncertain if they were ever legally married.

Pearl stayed in Canada just long enough to give birth to a son, then she quickly left the baby with her parents and headed for Phoenix, Arizona. Soon after, Frederick Hart tracked her down and convinced her it was time to settle down into a conventional life. Frederick took a job as a hotel manager in Phoenix and they lived a quiet life for five years or so, even adding a daughter to their little family. It is doubtful either was really content, and in 1898 Frederick left the family and enlisted in Teddy Roosevelt's Rough Riders and went off to fight in Cuba.

Pearl returned to her family in Canada, and in a repeat of her earlier actions, quickly left her children behind and headed off seeking new adventures, surfacing in various Arizona mining camps and taking whatever work she could find, legal or otherwise.

In 1899 Pearl hooked up with a miner named Joe Boot and told him she needed to raise money to help her sick mother back in Canada. The two hatched up a plan to rob the stagecoach that ran between Florence and Globe. The two neophyte desperadoes thought the job would be easy pickings.

As the stage rattled through the desert, Pearl and Joe stepped into its path with guns drawn and ordered the driver to stop. While Joe Boot guarded the driver, Pearl, dressed in men's clothes, ushered the stage's passengers out at gunpoint and relieved them of $450. Then they jumped on their horses and fired a warning shot and were off in a cloud of dust.

While the robbery went off as planned, neither Joe nor Pearl were experienced with anything that went on outside the boundaries of a boom town or mining camp. They quickly became lost and rode around in circles for a day or two until a posse caught up with them.

Lodged in the jail in Globe, Pearl played the role of lady outlaw to the hilt. Crowds gathered to see this petite and attractive woman outlaw, asking for her autograph. What bandit queen can be content sitting in a jail cell? Certainly not Pearl Heart, and within a week or two she and a prisoner named Ed Hogan escaped. Pearl had not learned anything about navigating the uncharted wilds of the Arizona frontier while incarcerated, and soon she was recaptured and taken back to jail. But the escape and subsequent manhunt helped spread her legend and solidified her self-proclaimed role of lady outlaw.

Pearl's trial was held in Florence, and it was obvious her romantic image had swayed public opinion in her favor. After deliberating a short time, the jury returned with an acquittal. Judge Doan was not nearly so taken with Pearl, and he quickly vacated the jury's verdict and empaneled a second jury, warning them not to be influenced by Pearl's gender and to concentrate on the facts of the case. This jury found the lady bandit guilty and she was sentenced to five years in the Territorial Prison in Yuma. Her partner in crime, Joe Boot, was sentenced to thirty years behind bars.

Pearl was one of 29 women who served time at the Territorial Prison over the years. She appears to have been a model prisoner, and after eighteen months she was paroled. Some stories say she was released because she became pregnant and the Arizona Territory did not want the scandal to become public knowledge.

Pearl went to Kansas City, where she attempted to cash in on her notoriety by playing herself in a stage drama of her life. Her fame lasted only a few weeks, then she dropped out of sight for a while. A year or so later she was arrested again, this time under the name Mrs. Keele, and charged with receiving stolen property. The next anyone heard of her was in 1924, when Pearl returned to Globe, Arizona and toured the old jail where she had been held years before.

From there Pearl's fate is a mystery. Some claim she married an Arizona rancher and lived out her days in a peaceful life where few knew of her past. Another story has her dying in San Francisco in 1925. No one really knows for sure. But one thing is certain, in the lore of the Old West, Arizona's Lady Bandit will live on forever.

Highway History And Back Road Mystery

Old Abe

Wisconsin's War Eagle

In a small park in Chippewa Falls, Wisconsin, we came across a monument to a bird that died 120 years ago. What does a bird do to deserve such recognition? Always intrigued by mysteries such as this, I had to look into the history behind the brass plaque to learn more. What I discovered was a fascinating historical tale.

Just as high schools and colleges often have mascots to boost team spirit and morale, military units sometimes adopt their own mascots. During the American Civil War, some military outfits had live bears, dogs, and even goats as mascots. But without a doubt, the most famous Civil War mascot was Old Abe, the Wisconsin War Eagle.

Chippewa Indians captured a baby eagle near present-day Park Falls in 1861, and a group of soldiers from the 8th Wisconsin Infantry Regiment, bound for service in Mississippi, bought him for $2.50. They promptly named their new pet Old Abe, after President

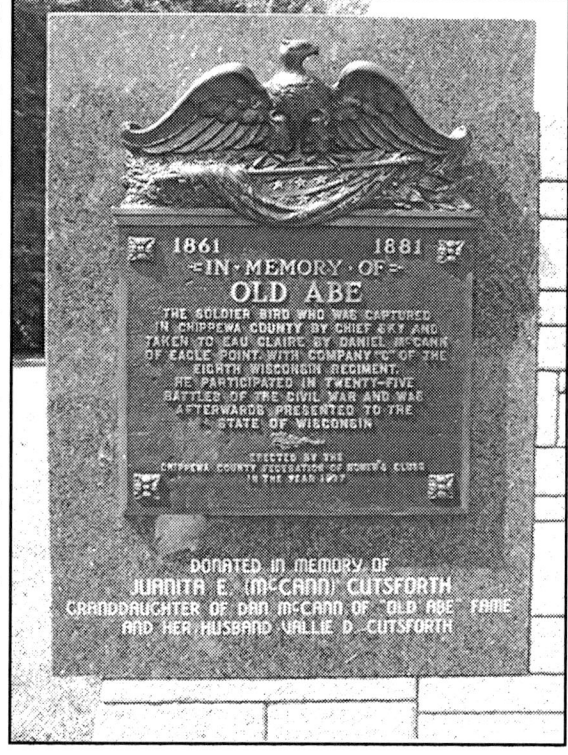

Highway History And Back Road Mystery

Abraham Lincoln, and ceremoniously swore him into military service. The eagle was draped with a red, white and blue ribbon and rosette, and seemed to be proud of his adornment. Captivated by their new mascot, the military unit promptly changed their nickname from the Badgers to the Eagles.

Old Abe was a hit with people everywhere he went. When the unit stopped in Chicago on their way south, crowds came to see him, and the *Chicago Tribune* newspaper carried a story about the eagle, calling him a "majestic bird."

The eagle's fame spread wherever his unit saw action. A soldier was always charged with caring for the bird during battle, and it is said that he was a good luck charm since not one of his caretakers was killed while tending Old Abe. It is reported that one of his soldier caretakers survived six battles, only to be killed in the next one after relinquishing his duty to another. Yet another story claims that during one skirmish, a wild shot tore harmlessly through Old Abe's feathers, scaring the bird so much that he leaped from his perch with enough force to drag his bearer off his feet, and a moment later a cannon ball landed in the exact spot where the soldier had been standing.

There are many tales told about Old Abe. How many are actually true are probably lost to the mists of time. Apparently the eagle was a bit of an adrenalin junky, and whenever the cannons roared and the muskets rattled, he was said to become very excited, hopping about on his perch and raising a terrible ruckus. Soldiers reported that on several occasions Old Abe actually sliced through his thick tether with his beak to take flight and soar high over the battlefield, screeching out encouragement to the Union soldiers.

At the Battle of Corinth, in Mississippi, Confederate General Sterling Price gave orders to his men to try to capture or kill the eagle, and though many a musket ball sailed in his direction as he flew over the rebel lines, seemingly taunting the enemy riflemen, Old Abe escaped unharmed. There were at least fifty different units engaged in the heated battle, yet Old Abe is said to have flown right through the smoke and bullets to land among his own Wisconsin

Highway History And Back Road Mystery

Eagle regiment.

The soldiers claimed that Old Abe got to where he could recognize different bugle calls, and whenever the signal to go into battle was sounded, he was ready to take to the air to oversee the action.

Perhaps the most impressive tale about Old Abe came after the siege of Vicksburg, at a nondescript little spot called Henderson's Hill. Rebel troops held the high ground, and the Wisconsin 8th was charged with taking it from them. The Union forces were afraid the enemy would be able to sneak a courier past their lines to summon reinforcements, trapping them between two lines of Confederate troops. Extra sentries were posted to intercept anyone attempting to cross their lines, but the northern soldiers did not spot any suspicious activity.

Suddenly Old Abe raised an alert with a raucous outcry, and soldiers sprang to their weapons just in time to catch a Confederate courier trying to slip past their lines to bring help to his besieged comrades. Realizing that reinforcements were not coming to their aid, eventually the Confederates surrendered, and Old Abe became known as "the bird who captured a fort."

As his fame spread, Old Abe attracted a lot of attention. Several other units attempted to purchase him, but his friends in the 8th Regiment would not part with their beloved mascot. Union General Sheridan visited the regiment to see the eagle, as did Ulysses S. Grant.

All told, Old Abe participated in over fifty major and minor engagements before the war ended, and though he got his tail feathers clipped by grape shot and musket balls a time or two, he came through the experience in one piece.

After the war, Old Abe was given a home in the Wisconsin State Capitol in Madison, living out his days in a special room reserved just for him, where many veterans and other visitors came to pay their respects to the old war bird. His fame continued to grow as newspaper accounts retold the tales of his exploits on the battlefield, and showman P.T. Barnum tried to buy the bird for $10,000, a huge sum in those days. But there was no way the people of Wisconsin were going to let their winged hero go.

Highway History And Back Road Mystery

Old Abe remained very much a character. When someone decided that he needed companionship, another eagle was introduced to his special room in the State Capitol. Old Abe promptly killed the intruder. However, when he was given a live rooster to eat, the old warrior instead made friends with it. When he took part in a parade in Pittsburgh honoring war veterans, riding in a handsome carriage drawn by four white horses for the five mile parade route, Old Abe is said to have squawked with delight at the crowds that cheered as he passed.

The guest of honor at many political affairs, Old Abe took advantage of the opportunities to bite both Generals Grant and Sherman. His old solder friends joked that "old Abe never really cottoned to generals." He apparently didn't cotton to political types very well either. One report said Old Abe, normally well mannered, was fond of soiling the fancy formal wear of visiting dignitaries.

In 1881, fifteen years after the war ended, Old Abe was living a comfortable life in the State Capitol when fire broke out. Though he was rescued from the flames, the proud old war bird died soon after from smoke inhalation. Mourned by Civil War veterans across the country, as well as his many other fans, Old Abe's body was stuffed and placed in a glass case in the Capitol, where he remained until another fire, in 1904, burned the Capitol down and he was lost in the flames.

Old Abe's memory and legacy live on. Today a replica of the stuffed eagle is perched in the Wisconsin Assembly Chambers. The Case Corporation, a Wisconsin-based machinery manufacturer, adopted Old Abe's image as their symbol in 1865. But perhaps Old Abe would be most proud of yet another symbolic representation. The Army's 101st Airborne Division, the famous Screaming Eagles, wear Old Abe's image on their shoulder patch, and the proud old war bird's silhouette has gone into battle with generations of young soldiers from World war II to Vietnam and the Gulf War. I like to think that Old Abe's spirit is still flying proudly over his troops wherever they may be called to go into battle even today.

Ohio And Michigan At War

Toledo War was a comedy of errors

It was, without a doubt, the most bizarre war that was never fought in American history. The elements that made up this conflict were a poorly surveyed boundary line, a hotheaded teenage governor, two "armies" that got lost and could not find each other to do battle, and a militia major who named his sons One and Two so he could remember which was the oldest. Though it sounds like the stuff of a Mel Brooks comedy, the Toledo War was a hotly contested issue back in 1835.

The trouble began with a survey done as part of the Northwest Ordinance of 1787. The ordinance set the southern boundary of Michigan Territory at a line drawn from the southern tip of Lake Michigan due east to Lake Erie. But there was a problem. The survey placed the southern tip of Lake Michigan further north than its actual location. This moved the boundary line further north than it should have been by all rights. But for years nobody noticed. Since Michigan was not yet a state and Ohio was, Ohio officials considered the territory as an unclaimed no mans land that they could annex at will. Ohio declared its boundary along a line north of the Maumee River, assuring the state access to Lake Erie, obviously a significant asset to have.

As Michigan's population grew and the territory began looking forward to statehood, the folks in Michigan also realized the benefits of controlling the mouth of the Maumee River (where present day Toledo sits) and a Lake Erie port. In 1818 Michigan officials ordered a new survey, which established the true boundary. The area between the two survey lines became known as the Toledo Strip. Confusion was the order of the day for people in the Toledo Strip. Mail was sometimes addressed to Ohio, other times to Michigan, and more often than not, did not arrive anyway. At least one frustrated writer sent a letter addressed to the "State of Confusion."

Not much happened for the next 15 years, but both sides kept a wary eye on the Toledo Strip, alert to any encroachment by the other. When Michigan petitioned Congress for statehood in 1835, the issue boiled to the surface again. Michigan's Territorial Governor, 19 year old Stephens T. Mason, appointed by none other than President Andrew Jackson, tried to negotiate the matter with Ohio officials, who laughed him out of the state.

Being young and typically quick to rile, Governor Mason assembled a force of militia and led them south to claim the Toledo Strip for Michigan. In April, 1835, Ohio Governor Robert Lucas responded by leading 300 of his own militiamen to Perrysburg, Ohio, just west of Toledo. For a few tense days it looked like the two forces would surely meet on the battlefield.

They probably would have, except for the fact that they could not find each other. Apparently neither governor was any better a navigator than he was a statesman, and the two groups spent a week floundering around lost in the swamps near Perrysburg before both sides gave up and withdrew without a shot being fired. The only casualties were several thousand mosquitos the hapless troopers killed to prevent being eaten alive, and possibly the egos of the two governors.

On April 26, Governor Lucas sent a survey party to Point Place, where they were met by a Michigan posse under Lenawee County Undersheriff William McNair. Harsh words were exchanged, threats thrown and guns drawn. This time several shots were fired, but again the inept "warriors" failed to do any damage, missing their targets on both sides.

The Michigan posse arrested the trespassers, and Governor Mason ordered his militia to search out and take any other Ohioans in the Toledo Strip prisoner. Among those captured were the family of Ohio Militia Major Benjamin Franklin Stickney. The humiliation of the major's arrest was compounded when the Michigan posse tied him to his horse for the trip to jail. Stickney had two sons, the oldest named One and the younger named Two. Young Two, enraged at his father's treatment, jumped forward and stabbed Monroe County Michigan Sheriff Joseph Wood in the thigh, drawing the only blood in the entire "war."

The longstanding dispute was resolved the next year when Congress, as a condition of granting Michigan statehood, made the new state surrender its claim to the Toledo Strip. As compensation for its loss, Michigan was awarded the vast and rich Upper Peninsula, a wild land rich in natural resources and recreational opportunities. Some people who have driven both Toledo's dirty congested streets and the uncrowded scenic byways of the Upper Peninsula say that Michigan got the better end of the bargain in the long run.

Highway History And Back Road Mystery

William Tell Kidnapped!

Located on the banks of the Ohio River, Tell City, Indiana is a pleasant little community of wide streets, modest homes with well trimmed lawns, and friendly small businesses. The city's downtown area is anchored by a handsome courthouse, with several monuments to area veterans. Standing atop a dry fountain in front of the courthouse is a life-size statue of Swiss folk hero William Tell, the archer who was challenged to shoot an apple off his own son's head by a tyrannical king. The statue is a tribute to Tell City's Swiss heritage and the hero the community was named after.

The story behind the statue is quite interesting. Back in 1974, local benefactor Austin Corbin commissioned the statue to commemorate the one hundredth anniversary of the town's founding.

Evansville, Indiana sculptor Don Ingle formed the statue of William Tell and his son, and the work was then shipped to a foundry in New York to be cast in bronze. When the call came that the work was completed, Ingle and his wife traveled to New York in a rented U-Haul van to pick up the 500 pound statue. The trip would prove to be eventful.

After spending the night in a motel in Ohio on the return trip,

Highway History And Back Road Mystery

the sculptor and his wife were horrified the next morning to discover that while they were sleeping, someone had stolen the van, with the statue inside it! With the statue's dedication scheduled for their arrival in Tell City, the statue must be found, and fast!

Frantic calls to the local police launched a massive manhunt (statue hunt?). Even the Federal Bureau of Investigation got into the act, and newspapers and broadcast news from coast to coast carried the story of the missing statue.

So how do you hide a 500 pound statue, anyway? Apparently the thief didn't know either, or maybe the heat was just too much to take. At any rate, he abandoned the van on a quiet side street in Cleveland, where a vigilant citizen discovered it, with William Tell inside. The recovered work of art continued on its trip to its new home, and today the statue of William Tell vigilantly stands guard over the courthouse lawn, one hand placed lovingly on his son's shoulder, the other carrying his crossbow over his shoulder. The folk hero appears none the worse for his unscheduled abduction, and ever since its installation at the courthouse, it has been a local landmark.

You will find the William Tell statue on the south side of Tell City's courthouse, overlooking the river and Main Street. Tell City is located on Indiana State Route 66, the Ohio River Scenic Byway, about halfway between Evansville and Louisville, Kentucky.

The Battle Of Picacho Pass

Driving along Interstate 10 between Tucson and Phoenix, Arizona, motorists cannot help but notice Picacho Peak, a rough volcanic spire jutting into the sky on the west side of the highway about fifty miles north of Tucson. Used as a landmark by explorers since as far back as the 17th Century, the peak helped guide Jesuit priest Father Kino as he brought Christianity to the Southwest, it was a guidepost for the De Anza Expedition in 1775, and for Forty-Niner fortune seekers on their way to the California gold fields. The pass through the peak was used by the Mormon Battalion on its way to California to fight in the war with Mexico, by Butterfield stagecoaches, and looked down on the first railroad as it pushed its way into the desert wilderness.

Besides being a noted landmark on the route between Arizona's two major metropolitan areas, Picacho Peak has a unique place in American history, for it was here that the western-most battle of the Civil War took place on April, 15, 1862.

When we think of the Civil War, most of us usually think of lines of blue and gray uniformed soldiers facing each other on the edge of some southern plantation, or maybe on the rolling green hills of Gettysburg. In truth, though the major battles were fought in the eastern half of the United States, there were skirmishes all across the country as Union supporters and Southern sympathizers met and clashed.

In the early days of the war the U.S. Army pulled its troops from duty protecting settlers in Arizona and sent them east to aid in the conflict. The Apache Indians quickly took advantage of the soldiers' withdrawal and went on the warpath, burning isolated ranches and threatening the tiny pueblo of Tucson.

The Confederacy saw an opportunity and wasted no time in exploiting it, dispatching troops to seize New Mexico Territory. Once the Rio Grande Valley was secure, Captain Sherrod Hunter was sent to Tucson to raise the Stars and Bars over the desert settlement. Hunter and his force of 75 men were welcomed by the citizens of Tucson, eager for any help they could find to help keep the Apaches at bay.

The seizure of the vast western frontier could not be tolerated, and the Union reacted quickly. Brigadier General James H. Carlton and his force of 1,400 troops that had been stationed in California set out from Fort Yuma to take Tucson away from the rebels. By early April General Carlton's California Column had reached present-day Casa Grande, Arizona. From there Carlton sent scouts to reconnoiter the route into Tucson.

Hearing of the Union advance, Captain Hunter sent out advance parties to head them off. They took up ambush positions on the rough hillsides of Picacho Pass and waited for the enemy to show up. From the pass the Confederate troops had a good view of the stage road the Union scouts would come up.

The Union cavalrymen recognized the threat potential of the pass and separated, one unit entering Picacho Pass, the other circling around to be in position if trouble started. At about 2 p.m. the scouts rode into range of Hunter's ambush and shots rang out. Two Union soldiers were injured and the rest took cover. Almost immediately the second detachment attacked the Confederate skirmish line, capturing three men.

Union Lieutenant James Barrett led a charge against the Confederate position, who responded with heavy fire. Barrett and three of his men were killed, and a couple of others wounded. The Union troops withdrew to cover and the two sides traded shots until darkness fell, under cover of which the Union troops returned to join the main body of the California Column waiting at Casa Grande.

Thus ended the battle, but it was a hollow victory for the Confederates. Captain Hunter's men were outnumbered and too far away from Confederate lines to receive reinforcements and supplies. By the time the California Column arrived in Tucson, Hunter and his men had retreated to New Mexico. Their trek was a harsh one, under constant attack by Apaches, to the point where it became such a matter of survival that they even armed their Union prisoners to have enough firepower to make it to safety. They arrived at the Rio Grande on May 27, 1862, ragged and beaten. The Confederate occupation of Arizona was over.

These days Picacho Peak is home to a state park with 100 camping sites, some with partial hookups, a dump station, picnic tables, ramadas, restrooms and showers. The park includes hiking trails, a playground, and historical markers remembering the battle that took place here.

Every year there is a re-enactment of the Battle of Picacho Pass in early March. Over 200 history enthusiasts in period uniforms establish Union and Confederate camps and do battle before crowds of delighted visitors. The annual event is popular and brings out large crowds, who come to enjoy the beauty of the desert in Spring and cheer on the combatants.

Picacho Peak State Park's hiking trails vary in difficulty. The two mile Hunter Trail, rated as difficult, begins on the north side from Barrett Loop and leads to the top of the peak. The trial is steep and twisting, with steel cables anchored in places to assist hikers make it over the more difficult spots.

The Sunset Vista Trail, just over three miles long, starts at the westernmost parking lot on the south side of the park and leads to the top of Picacho Peak. The trail is moderate for the first two miles or so, then becomes a hard climb.

For easier to manage explorations, consider the Calloway Trail, 3/4 of a mile that leads to a scenic overlook; the half mile Nature Trail; or the short Children's Cave Trail. The latter two include interpretive signs along their routes.

Picacho Peak itself is the eroded plug of an extinct volcano. This is rough country, and summer temperatures can soar to well over one hundred degrees. Be sure to bring plenty of water. The peak's sides are covered with a myriad of vegetation, including blue lupine, brittlebush, rare albino poppies, creosote, and cacti. Visitors may spot mule deer, desert tortoise, lizards, snakes (including rattlesnakes), Gila monsters, coyote, and many species of birds.

Besides the state park campground, there are a couple of privately owned campgrounds nearby. An interesting side trip during your visit to Picacho Peak State Park is Rooster Cogburn's Ostrich Ranch at the base of the mountain along the Interstate 10 frontage road. The operation is home to hundreds of ostriches raised for their meat and eggs.

Picacho Peak State Park is located at exit 219 off Interstate 10. The exit also provides access to the ostrich ranch, RV parks, and a scattering of local businesses. For more information on Picacho Peak State Park, call 520-466-3183.

A Family Obligation

The long, horrible war was finally over, and the weary men of the 70th Ohio Infantry Regiment were headed home. These battle-hardened men had seen the worst war had to offer, including the Atlanta Campaign and Sherman's March to the Sea. They had survived cannon shells, Rebel bayonets, disease and deprivation. Some were recently freed from Andersonville Prison, the notorious hell hole where thousands of Union soldiers had died under terrible conditions.

Now it was August, 21, 1865, and the Union soldiers were nearing home, transported up the mighty Ohio River on the 155 foot long steamboat *Argosy III*. Little did they know that their ordeal was far from over.

Nearing Rono Landing (now renamed Magnet), Indiana a strong storm came up, drenching the soldiers with driving rain. Many crowded around the overloaded boat's boiler for shelter from the wind and rain. Suddenly a severe wind gust drove the *Argosy III* into the shore and her paddlewheel became mired in the mud.

Almost immediately the boiler exploded, scalding the soldiers gathered around with steam and hot water. Panic-stricken, many jumped into the river to escape. Ten soldiers died in the accident, either drowned or scalded to death. Their comrades managed to pull them to shore, and soon another passing boat stopped to render assistance, carrying some of the most badly injured upriver to Louisville, Kentucky. People living in Rono offered what aid and comfort they could. It was one of those terrible ironies that cannot be explained, one more injustice heaped upon men who had already suffered far too much. The ten men who perished in the accident were buried in a mass grave, and for nearly a century the tragedy was forgotten as the country worked to recover from the Civil War.

In 1963 a Perry County, Indiana resident named Forrest McNaughton mentioned hearing something from his parents many years before about some Civil War soldiers being killed in a shipwreck near Rono. The story intrigued a local doctor, who began writing letters to the Department of the Army and the General Services Administration seeking information on the incident. Over time Doctor Current managed to piece together the story of the tragedy.

In 1965 a farmer from Magnet named Clyde Benner decided it was appropriate to honor the dead men, and he placed a monument on his land overlooking the accident site. The monument's ten vertical headstones carry the names of nine of the soldiers who died here, and one who could be identified only as "Unknown US Soldier."

For the rest of his life, Clyde Benner tended the small plot of land, mowing and trimming around the markers and clearing a space where visitors could pause and reflect on the sacrifices of these men.

After Benner passed away in 1994, his daughter Pat Irvin and her family took over the chore, assisted by Pat's three sisters. They have added a split-rail fence, and today the family still cares for the grave site, nestled in a grove of trees by the side of the road a half mile or so upriver from Magnet. It is a family obligation owed to men who gave their all for their nation. Here in southern Indiana, obligations are not easily forgotten.

Highway History And Back Road Mystery

Highway History And Back Road Mystery

The Mystery Of Lady Bountiful

The busy small town of Livingston, in Polk County, Texas is best known for nearby Lake Livingston, with its many fishing and recreational opportunities, and as the home of the huge Escapees RV Club, an organization of thousands of folks who travel and live either full or part time in recreational vehicles. Situated in the piney woods of east Texas, and serviced by two U.S. Highways, the Livingston of today is far removed from the small settlement where Wisconsin lumber baron Will Knox brought his family in 1900, establishing a sawmill on 10,000 acres of timberland he had purchased.

The Knox family – Will, his wife Mary, the couple's son Hiram and his wife Grace, along with their son Willie settled near Livingston for a time, then purchased an additional 25,000 acres of timber near Hemphill, in Sabine County. Both operations were successful and the family was soon established as leaders in their community.

In those days, transportation was not nearly as speedy or comfortable as we enjoy today. Roads were rough trails at best, and a journey of 100 miles could take days. On a business trip to Houston, Hiram Knox was stricken with pneumonia and spent several weeks recuperating before he was strong enough to make the somewhat arduous journey home. While he was ill, an attractive young woman named Lillian Marshall nursed him back to health. Appreciative of her help and captivated by her winning personality, the entire Knox family soon came to love the young nurse. She became a part of the family, almost an adopted daughter.

Tragically, Hiram's wife became seriously ill soon after he

returned from Houston, and died unexpectedly. Grief-stricken, Hiram turned to the lovely young woman, who was there to comfort him just as she had while he was sick with pneumonia. He found solace in her arms, and after a suitable grieving period, Hiram and Lillian were married.

For a time, life was good for the Knox family. Their business continued to thrive and Lillian fit right into the family. But there was more sorrow to come, and it did not wait long. A year after his mother's death, Hiram's son Willie was murdered under mysterious conditions, and his slayer was never caught.

Hiram Knox was not the only member of his family to come under Lillian's spell. While she soon came to dominate her husband, her father-in-law was enamored by her beauty and appreciated the fact that she plunged head-on into the family business, learning every aspect of the operation. At times she would travel out of town with the elder Knox on business trips.

By 1913 the family was expanding its business again, building a new sawmill in a settlement they established called East Mayfield, in Sabine County. But the tragedy that seemed to attach itself to the Knox family was not finished yet. Not by a long shot. While on a business trip to Houston, family patriarch Will Knox suddenly fell ill and died.

Though devastated by so many losses in such a short time, Hiram, with Lillian's stalwart assistance, plunged himself back into the business and finished the new sawmill. Under Lillian's direction, the couple built a home that can only be described as a palace. Built by fine craftsmen, adorned with exotic woods and the most expensive fixtures, decorated with lavish furniture, imported tapestries, and expensive works of art, no expense was spared to create the home. Stables held Arabian horses, garages were erected for a fleet of fancy automobiles, and even a private zoo was included on the grounds!

While Hiram never seemed to have his father's vision or his wife's drive, Lillian excelled at business and soon controlled every aspect of the family enterprise. Under her guidance the company ran a short line railroad, and she personally supervised the logging operation.

Highway History And Back Road Mystery

Lillian clearly loved her role as timber baroness, and by most reports was a benevolent ruler of her own little kingdom. She treated her employees and their families very well, personally nursed sick and injured women and children, and lavished expensive gifts on the community. So well known in her industry was Lillian that in 1918 the *American Lumberman* magazine called her "the most remarkable woman in the lumber industry." The people of East Mayfield had a more affectionate title for Lillian Knox – Lady Bountiful. There is no doubt that she was loved and adored by many.

But there were always a few skeptics who wondered about the sudden deaths that had plagued the Knox family after Lillian came into the picture, and their suspicions were raised anew when Hiram Knox was found shot to death in his bed on November 26, 1922. He held a pistol, and had left goodbye letters to his mother and attorney, but Sheriff George Alford was not convinced this was a simple suicide.

Several clues led the sheriff to suspect foul play. George was shot in the back of the head, not the temple or mouth, as most suicides happen. In addition, there were no powder burns on the head, which are left when a firearm is used at close range. Mysterious footprints found outside the bedroom raised more red flags. The sheriff charged Lillian Knox with the murder of her husband.

Perhaps it was lack of evidence, or maybe Lillian's good reputation in the community helped, but whatever the reason was, a grand jury refused to indict her, ruling only that Hiram Knox had died at the hands of an unknown assassin.

Even though she was not tried in her husband's death, the incident seemed to be a turning point for Lillian. The family business began to sour, and before long she left the area. But more mystery was to cloud her life. In 1937 she was questioned, along with her oldest son, in the beating death of the last of the Knox family, Mary Knox, who was killed in Dallas. Again, though suspected, Lillian was not indicted for the murder.

Her good name ruined, Lillian disappeared from Texas. Using a series of aliases, Lillian roamed as far as Chicago, where she was implicated in several fraud cases in the 1950s. She eventually served four years in prison for mail fraud. Lady Bountiful, the Baroness of Sabine County, had fallen a long way from the days when she ruled a successful lumber company and lived in the finest home in the region.

In 1966, at the age of 75, Lillian died in a mental hospital in Illinois. She was buried in a pauper's grave, and none of her nine children were on hand to see her laid to rest. She took to her grave any secrets she may have had about the mysterious deaths that had destroyed the Knox family that had taken her in and allowed her to rise from nurse to princess.

Highway History And Back Road Mystery

Abe Lincoln Goes To Court

Most of us associate Abraham Lincoln with the state of Illinois, but actually our sixteenth president was born in Kentucky and spent much of his early years in Indiana. Several locations in the southern portion of the Hoosier State have references to the time Lincoln spent here. Just west of the small Ohio River town of Troy on State Route 66 is Lincoln Ferry State Wayside Park, one such location that played a part of the future president's life.

When he was sixteen, young Abe went to work for a farmer and entrepreneur named James Taylor. In his later years, Lincoln would recall this as some of the hardest work he ever did - butchering hogs, plowing, and splitting fence rails.

One of the chores assigned to Abe was operating a small boat used to ferry passengers across Anderson River, which empties into the Ohio. Always looking for an opportunity, young Abraham Lincoln realized that if people would pay to cross small Anderson River, they would also pay for a ride out to the river boats and barges that worked the river. He already had contacts with the river boats, since he had begun a sideline business cutting firewood to power their steam boilers, selling it for fifty cents a cord.

The enterprising teenager built himself a rowboat and began carrying passengers out to the river boats. On his first trip he carried two passengers, who paid him $1 for his services. Never one you could call a dunce, the teenager quickly realized that making twice as much money as he did for cutting firewood, with a lot less work involved, was a winning idea. Soon he was kept busy rowing passengers and crew members out to passing boats in the river.

It wasn't long before trouble followed. At that time the state of

Highway History And Back Road Mystery

Kentucky claimed jurisdiction over the Ohio River, and had issued a pair of brothers with the last name of Dill a license to ferry passengers across the river. The brothers filed charges against young Mr. Lincoln, and Abe was hauled into court in Lewisport, Kentucky.

Even at that young age, Abraham Lincoln's keen mind was at work. He read the law giving Kentucky the right to rule over the Ohio River, and studied the agreement between the Dill brothers and the state of Kentucky, granting them the exclusive right to ferry passengers across the river.

Imagine the court's surprise when this tall, lanky youngster from the other side of the river declared he intended to defend himself. There were more surprises in store! Abe argued that the Dill's agreement granted them the right to ferry passengers *across* the Ohio River. He claimed that he had never ferried anyone across the river, he had only rowed passengers to boats *in* the river, so he was not in competition with the Dills! He had never violated their exclusive right to ferry passengers *across* the river! The court had to agree, and Abraham Lincoln walked out of court with all charges dismissed and free to continue to row passengers in his little boat.

That experience in court no doubt sparked Abe's interest in the law, and while Indiana ended up losing a pretty good ferryman, the country got a pretty decent attorney and later an excellent president out of the deal!

Today Lincoln Ferry Wayside Park marks the spot at the mouth of the Anderson River where young Abe Lincoln operated his ferry business and got his first taste of both private enterprise and the legal profession. The park includes a small pavilion and parking area, with great views of the stretch of Ohio River where young Abe Lincoln spent his days carrying passengers in his little handmade rowboat.

Andersonville

The South's most notorious prison camp

If war is hell, as the saying goes, then prisoners of war must suffer in an even more unbearable level of hell. Imagine what it must be like for a terrified soldier engaged in battle to find himself at the mercy of the very people he was trying to kill only moments before. The people who were trying just as hard to kill him! They say that freedom has a taste that only those who have fought for it can ever truly know. I think that taste must be especially sweet for those who once lost their freedom to an armed enemy.

Today international treaties and world opinion molded by mass communications hopefully assure prisoners of war humane treatment, though there is never any guarantee when taken by a hostile force. In times past, prisoner treatment was often harsh and severe. In the days of the Civil War there were certain standards that were expected in prisoner treatment, but those standards were unmet more often than not.

Camp Sumter, located near the tiny Georgia town of Andersonville, was one of the largest Confederate military prisons. During the fourteen months the prison was operating, more than 45,000 Union soldiers were confined at Andersonville. Of those, almost 13,000 died from disease, malnutrition, poor sanitation, overcrowding and exposure to the elements. To bring that number into more understandable terms, that is a rate of over 30 men a day, every day for fourteen months. One death every 48 minutes, 24 hours a day, seven days a week. Even today the pastoral rolling hills of Andersonville cannot hide the aura of the suffering and death experienced here.

Early in the war the custom was to release captured prisoners back to their own ranks through prisoner exchanges or pardons. Exchanged prisoners capable of service usually went back into battle, sometimes without even a short recuperation leave. Pardoned prisoners were expected, on their word of honor, not to engage in battle against their former captors, tough they often served in non-combatant roles. As the war dragged on, Confederate leaders realized that their best chance to even the odds against the larger, better equipped Union armies was to hold their prisoners instead of releasing them to fight again.

The fatal flaw in this plan was that the ever-growing number of prisoners placed a severe strain on the South's resources. They had to be fed, housed, and guarded by an embattled nation that did not have enough to feed and shelter their own soldiers and civilians, or enough troops to fill the battle lines. It is not surprising that prisoners were a low priority for Confederate leaders.

The original prison covered about sixteen acres enclosed by a fifteen foot high stockade hewn from pine logs. It was soon enlarged to over 26 acres to accommodate the growing numbers of prisoners who poured in on prisoner trains daily. The stockade was 1,620 feet long and 779 feet wide, with sentry boxes placed every thirty feet. Inside the prison, about nineteen feet from the wall, was the "dead line." Prisoners were forbidden to cross the dead line, and anyone who did so was immediately shot. There were two entrances to the prison, the North and South Gates, both of which were located on the west wall. Outside the stockade, eight small earthen forts were spread around the prison and armed with cannon to put down any riot or insurrection inside the compound and as defense against Union cavalry attack. A small stream called Stockade Branch flowed through the prison and supplied water.

The first prisoners arrived at Andersonville in February 1864, and over the next few months they poured in at the rate of 400 a day. By the end of June the prison that was originally built to house 10,000 men held some 26,000 captives. The prisoner population swelled past 32,000 in August 1864. The prison cadre was quickly overwhelmed and realized there was no way to adequately care for this many men.

Highway History And Back Road Mystery

Trying unsuccessfully to cope with a quickly deteriorating economy, an inadequate transportation system, and the need to concentrate all available resources to the war effort, the South was completely unprepared and incapable of taking care of their prisoners.

Conditions were harsh on the best of days at Andersonville. With scant food and clothing and little or no shelter, the Union prisoners endured broiling summer heat, bone-chilling nights, rain and wind. The waters of Stockade Creek were quickly polluted with waste and dysentery ran rampant through the prisoner population.

What food there was consisted of slim rations of rice, beans and cornmeal, most of very poor quality and contaminated with parasites. Most of the rations contained too much fiber, making it indigestible. There was no formal food service, every man had to fend for himself. What firewood there was to begin with was soon exhausted.

Life under such circumstances was tenuous at best for the prisoners. Filth and disease went hand in hand. The smallest cut or scrape could quickly lead to infection that often resulted in death. Diseases such as tuberculosis, gangrene, and dysentery took a terrible toll, and the prison's tiny hospital, with no medicines or supplies, was not capable of doing anything except being a place to die. Suffering was the only existence the prisoners knew, and the death rate began to climb. The bodies of the dead were stacked in a death house outside the stockade and buried nearby.

The prisoners did what they could to survive, digging wells inside the compound with pocket knives, sticks and their bare hands. They erected crude shelters called shebangs from blankets or coats and sticks, huddling under them for shelter from the sun or to ward off the cold. Prisoners soon learned that there was strength in numbers and banded together in small groups to help each other survive. Some of the wells the prisoners dug were actually escape tunnels. While quite a few prisoners managed to crawl out of the stockade through these tunnels, most were soon captured and returned to the prison.

People are not always honorable, and there will always be those who will seek to profit on the misery of others. Andersonville was no exception. A group of prisoners called the Raiders began preying on their fellow prisoners, beating them and robbing them of their possessions, food, and even their clothing. Through intimidation and terror they managed to bully the other prisoners until there was a minor revolt and the prisoners demanded help from their guards. Captain Henry A. Wirz, in command of the prison, ordered trials for the Raiders, with prisoners serving as jurors. Convicted, many Raiders were forced to run a gauntlet of the prisoners who rained down blows upon them as punishment. The six ringleaders of the Raiders were ordered executed.

Captain Wirz, though vilified for the conditions that existed at Andersonville, was as much a victim of circumstance as his prisoners. Placed in charge of the prison, he received no support from the Confederate government to care for his charges. Camp records and the testimony of most of the prisoners who survived Andersonville agree that Wirz did what he could to ease conditions, but his efforts were crippled by a lack of supplies and superiors who turned a deaf ear to his requests for aid.

With the advance of Union General William T. Sherman's forces, who occupied Atlanta on September 2, 1864, Federal cavalry was now within striking distance of Andersonville. Confederate authorities, worried that the prisoners might be liberated and able to return to the fight, moved most of the prisoners to camps in South Carolina and coastal Georgia. Andersonville continued to operate on a scaled down basis until the end of the war.

When the war ended and word of the suffering in Andersonville reached the people up North, the public cried out for revenge. Captain Wirz was charged with conspiring with Confederate officials to "impair and injure the health and destroy the lives of his prisoners" and "murder in violation of the laws of war." Though there was never a conspiracy, Wirz was the whipping boy who bore the guilt for circumstances beyond his control. He was convicted and executed in Washington, D.C. on November 10, 1865. Today a monument to Captain Wirz, erected by the Georgia Division of the United Daughters of the Confederacy, stands in the town of Andersonville.

The prison officially closed in May of 1865, and in July of the same year Clara Barton came to the prison's cemetery with a detachment of laborers and soldiers on orders of President Abraham Lincoln to identify and mark the graves of the Union dead, and to gather information on missing soldiers so their families could know their fate. Barton was assisted by a former prisoner named Dorence Atwater, who had been assigned to record the names of prisoners who died while at Andersonville for Confederate records. Fearful that the records might disappear or be destroyed at the end of the war, Atwater kept his own secret copy to help identify some 12,000 dead interred at the cemetery. Atwater's list and Confederate records captured at the end of the war managed to identify all but 460 graves at Andersonville. Those graves were marked simply Unknown US Soldier. Today the cemetery is a National Cemetery, and burials of service members and veterans are still held at Andersonville. Every year on Veterans Day every grave in the cemetery is honored with a small American flag, with the exception of six graves, those of the Andersonville Raiders executed for their crimes against their fellow prisoners.

The prison site came into private ownership in 1875. In 1890 it was purchased by the Georgia Department of the Grand Army of the Republic (GAR), a Union veterans organization. The group sold the property to the Woman's Relief Corps, the national auxiliary of the GAR, for $1. The Woman's Relief Corps made many improvements to the site with the intention of creating a memorial park. Northern states began erecting commemorative monuments to their sons who died at Andersonville. In 1910 the Woman's Relief Corps donated the prison site to the people of the United States. Andersonville was administered by the Department of the Army until designated a National Historic Site in 1971, when it came under the province of the National Park Service.

Today Andersonville National Historic Site is a 495 acre park that includes the old prison site, the National Cemetery, and the National Prisoner of War Museum. Park rangers lead guided tours through the old prison grounds, pointing out sections of the stockade wall that have been reconstructed, the sites of wells dug by the prisoners as they tried to obtain water, and telling visitors about the terrible ordeal prisoners faced on this ground so long ago. White posts define the dead line over which prisoners could not stray without being shot by alert guards.

Andersonville was not the only hell hole where prisoners suffered during the Civil War, and inhuman conditions were not confined to the South. Confederate prisoners held in Ohio and Illinois also perished under poor conditions, but not to the extent they did at Andersonville. But history is written by the victors, and Andersonville became synonymous with terrible treatment of war prisoners.

The National Prisoner of War Museum at Andersonville is a memorial to all America prisoners of war from any era. Opened in 1998, the museum tells of the sacrifice and courage of American prisoners of war from the Revolution to the Gulf War.

Exhibits in the museum include artifacts from prisoners of all wars, multimedia displays and dioramas. One display shows a crude bamboo structure such as those used to house American POWs in Southeast Asia, while another is of a shackled prisoner in solitary confinement. The stories of prisoners include tales of brutality, torture, starvation, and the human spirit that gave them the strength to survive. In a heart-wrenching video, former prisoners of war and their families relate their experiences of capture, endurance, hope, and homecoming. A computer database at the museum lists Union prisoners of war and Confederate guards at Andersonville. Touring the museum is an emotional experience where we can begin to understand the suffering and sacrifice of our country's prisoners of war, and come away with a new appreciation of their experience.

Andersonville National Historic Site is located ten miles northeast of Americus, Georgia on State Route 49, and is open daily. For more information on Andersonville, write Andersonville National Historic Site, 496 Cemetery Road, Andersonville, Georgia 31711, or call 229-924-0343. The site can be visited on the World Wide Web at www.nps.gov/ande.

America's Stonehenge

On a few acres of granite hillside in Salem, New Hampshire sits a mysterious collection of rock walls and structures that have mystified historians and archaeologists for ages. No one knows who created this maze of chambers, ceremonial places, and astronomical alignments, but its ancient builders were obviously well versed in both astronomy and stone construction. The site is an accurate astronomically aligned calendar and to this day can be used to determine specific solar and lunar events of the year.

The secrets of its origin are lost in time, but America's Stonehenge has revealed many clues to its history. Archaeological excavations have uncovered an amazing range of historic and prehistoric artifacts, ranging from stone tools, pottery, and ancient Old World scripts to eighteenth and nineteenth century housewares and implements. Excavation of a fire pit has revealed evidence of humans at the site over 7,000 years ago. It is believed the site once served as a stop on the Underground Railroad, and digs at Stonehenge have revealed manacles believed to have been removed from fugitive slaves in the 1830s and 1840s.

Some think America's Stonehenge was built by an ancient Native American culture who used it as a place of ceremony and sacrifice. Others believe a mysterious race of migrant Europeans may be responsible. Whoever it was, their achievements are remarkable when you consider the crude construction practices and technology of their time. This is most likely the oldest man-made construction in the United States. There are several other similar sites in New England of the same mysterious origin, but the New Hampshire site is the largest and best documented.

America's Stonehenge opened to the public under the name Mystery Hill Caves in 1958. In 1982 the name was changed to America's Stonehenge to better reflect what is believed is the true origin of the site. Over the years exploration and excavation have continued to try to unlock its mysteries.

A tour of America's Stonehenge begins at the Visitor Center, where artifacts unearthed in the site's various excavations are displayed. The Visitor Center has a small theater where you can watch an interesting video on the site.

From the Visitor Center, a marked trail leads uphill to the Main Site. This trail is not suitable for those in wheelchairs or who have difficulty walking. Along the way, stop and visit with the three resident alpacas. Cousins to the llama, alpacas were domesticated in South America about 5,000 years ago to provide fine clothing for Inca royalty. Following the Spanish Conquest, the animals nearly became extinct, and it was not until the mid-1800s that the qualities of alpaca fleece were rediscovered and the animals began to make a comeback.

The Main Site is only a portion of a complex series of walls and structures at America's Stonehenge. At one time a settler named Jonathan Pattee had a home here, and used part of the old stone walls as a foundation for his cabin. Pattee used some of the stone chambers for storage. Unfortunately, he also modified some of the walls to meet his needs during his occupation of the area. At one time a quarry also operated at the site, and it is feared important structures may have been destroyed during this period as well.

Researchers have been able to differentiate between the original structures and Pattee's work, and signs along the trails identify significant points of interest. Among these are one eight ton slab that is believed to have served as a roof for one or more chambers. A cutout at the bottom of the slab is believed to have been used as a levering point to move the massive stone slab. Another stone slab has a hole bored at 90 degrees through it at one edge, and may have been used as a gate post, similar to ones found in Malta, though its actual purpose is unknown.

Many of the structures show what may be a European influence. A set of stone steps excavated in 1955 were believed to have led down into a courtyard surrounded by several structures that have disappeared over time. In Europe such arrangements were called Megaron Areas.

One of the most interesting structures at the site is the Oracle Chamber, with its Speaking Tube and Secret Bed. Words spoken through the stone-lined Speaking Tube exit outside the chamber under the Sacrificial Table. Below the Speaking Tube is the Secret Bed, a rock niche large enough for a person to crawl into and be completely hidden, but still able to observe all activity through a small hidden opening near the floor. What ancient soothsayer may have used this chamber? Across from the Speaking Tube and Secret Bed is a seat of bedrock estimated at 45 tons that was split and moved from the opposite wall of the chamber. To sit in the dark on this seat and ponder the significance of this chamber and speculate on what may have happened here long ago is quite an experience.

Outside the Oracle Chamber is the nearly five ton Sacrificial Table, a grooved slab whose purpose is still debated by researchers. It is believed to have been used for sacrifices, due to its location above the Speaking Tube and the carved channel that would carry away blood.

Highway History And Back Road Mystery

The three section East-West Chamber is the only chamber at the site that does not have a south-facing opening. This chamber is similar to ancient European structures, and may have some astronomical significance. Some believe that it was used as a galley grave.

From a viewing platform constructed in 1975, you can see the major astronomical alignments of the different walls and strategically placed stones. Included in these are stones for true north alignments and winter and summer solstice sunrises and sunsets.

From the Main Site, a path leads to the Astronomical Trail, a series of stone walls and monolithic astronomical alignments that continue to amaze modern scientists for their accuracy. These structures range in age from 1500 B.C. to 650 A.D. and are a testament to the skill and knowledge of the mysterious people who built America's Stonehenge. We may never know who these ancient engineers were, but just to see the remains of their work is an experience to be remembered.

America's Stonehenge is located in Salem, New Hampshire, about thirty miles north of Boston, Massachusetts, and is open daily except for Thanksgiving and Christmas Days. For more information, call 603-893-8300, write them at America's Stonehenge, P.O. Box 84, Salem, New Hampshire 03073, or visit their website at www.stonehengeusa.com

Rails Over The Water
A Visit To The S.S. City of Milwaukee

In the late 1800s, industry in the Midwest faced a major obstacle if it was to grow. Goods and materials shipped by railroad faced long delays, usually a week or more, passing through the heavily congested rail yards in Chicago. Time was money, and millions of dollars were lost every year while cargos sat idle in box cars waiting to work their way through the system at the overworked railroad center. Railroads and shippers knew they had to find a way to speed up the process of getting goods across the water barrier that Lake Michigan presented.

Earliest efforts to move railroad freight across Lake Michigan involved unloading a train's cargo into a ship, crossing the lake, and loading the cargo onto another train. While still faster than running a train around the lake through Chicago, there had to be a better way.

The first step in solving the problem was taken on November 27, 1892 with the launching of the *Ann Arbor No. 1*, the first of what would grow to be a powerful fleet of train carferries, capable of carrying up to 30 railroad cars across Lake Michigan in a matter of hours, rather than the weeks wasted in going around the bottom of the lake by rail. The ships backed up to a dock and opened a special gate that matched up with railroad tracks on the dock, and railroad cars were backed right onto rails in the ship's train deck. Once at their destination, the ship was again backed up to a special dock with railroad tracks, and the train cars were moved ashore. The process greatly sped up the time involved in transporting cargo across the lake.

For the next 100 years several companies operated carferries across Lake Michigan. During their busiest period there were fifteen

Highway History And Back Road Mystery

different ferry routes carrying railroad cars and passengers from ports in Michigan to Wisconsin and back. The carferries represented a special era in lake commerce, one that combined the romance of luxury ocean liner travel with the most efficient method of transporting industrial goods and materials.

The carferries operated year round, braving the very worst weather Lake Michigan could produce. Enduring crashing waves, high winds, and dense ice were all part of the job for these strong ships and the hardy men who sailed aboard them. Ice was a ship's worst enemy, capable of stopping her in her path, crushing steel hulls, or building up on a ship's deck until it weighed her down and sent her crashing to the bottom. It is a tribute to the men who built the carferries and the men who sailed on them that in over 100 years of service in all kinds of weather, only three of the vessels were lost at sea.

Changing economics in the railroad industry and more efficient methods of getting rail cars through the bottleneck in Chicago eventually put the carferries out of business. The last railroad carferry run was made by the *S.S. Badger*, leaving Kewaunee, Wisconsin and docking in Ludington, Michigan in November 1990.

After their service some of the ships were converted for other use and many were eventually scrapped. Today only one of the former carferries remains in active service. The *S.S. Badger* is now operated by Lake Michigan Carferry Service, carrying passengers and automobiles between Ludington, Michigan and Manitowoc, Wisconsin during the summer months. Transporting railroad cars across Lake Michigan on carferries is no longer economically feasible.

The last remaining traditional Great Lakes carferry, the *S.S. City of Milwaukee*, is now on display in Manistee, Michigan. A National Historic Landmark, the ship is open for tours, giving visitors the opportunity to learn about the proud history of the ship and her sister vessels. Very knowledgeable tour guides lead visitors throughout the ship, including places below decks that passengers were never allowed to see during the *City of Milwaukee's* working days.

The *City of Milwaukee* was launched on November 25, 1930,

the last of six sister ships built to plans developed by the Manitowoc Shipbuilding Company. The steel-hulled vessel measures 348 feet long and was powered by twin triple expansion engines that could move her along at 14 knots and had the force to crush through three feet of solid Great Lake ice. The ship's train deck could hold an entire 30 boxcar train on four tracks.

The *City of Milwaukee* was built to replace the *S.S. Milwaukee*, another carferry that was lost with all hands in a violent storm on

October 22, 1929. *Milwaukee* departed Milwaukee, Wisconsin into the teeth of a strong gale with winds clocked up to 37 miles an hour. Bound for Grand Haven, Michigan, the trip would have taken only a few hours under normal conditions. But when she had not arrived within 48 hours officials on shore feared the worst. Either *Milwaukee* had detoured north to hide in the lee of the coastline somewhere, or she was lost. Days later a Coast Guard sailor near South Haven, Michigan found a message in a waterproof container written by *Milwaukee's* purser. The message outlined the vessel's last hours: *The ship is taking on water fast. We have turned around and headed for Milwaukee. Pumps are working but sea gate is bent and can't*

keep the water out. Seas are tremendous. Things look bad....

    City of Milwaukee was involved in Lake Michigan train ferry service for all of her working life, retiring in operating condition in 1981. During her active days *City of Milwaukee* was operated by Grand Trunk Milwaukee Ferry Company, but was leased to other railroads at one time or another, giving her a historic connection with each of the Great Lakes Carferry Fleets.

    The ship is a wonderful example of life on the Great Lakes. While the work was hard, the crew and passengers enjoyed many modern amenities not usually found in ships of that day. The galley, where meals were prepared, included a freezer where ice cream and other treats were stored. The *City of Milwaukee* could carry up to 300 passengers, as well as the boxcars in her cargo hold. Passengers dined in style, served by white-jacketed waiters. During the lake crossing they could relax in staterooms that resembled railroad Pullman cars, or spend their time in the grand salon, decorated with wonderful oak paneling and fine appointments. A glass-fronted observation room offered great views of the lake. After dinner male passengers often retired to the smoking room, where they enjoyed a cigar and a drink while they discussed the day's events. The wheelhouse, with all of its polished brass, featured the latest nautical technology.

    Below decks, the engine crew lived in the "flicker" quarters near their duty station, where a round-the-clock card game usually went on under sporadic electric light, hence the name flicker. Just outside the flicker was the train deck.

    The massive railroad cars had to be locked securely once aboard ship, to prevent any movement in heavy seas. Even one inch of slack could allow the heavily loaded cars to break free and wreak disaster. Crews worked on four hour watches while at sea, except during storms, when every hand was on duty to help the vessel stay afloat. During nasty winter weather it was common for crew members to be dispatched to the slippery decks to chop ice loose with axes. Loading and unloading kept the entire crew busy getting the passengers and cargo aboard and secured.

    Life aboard the *City of Milwaukee* had its highlights. Humor

Highway History And Back Road Mystery

seems to have been a great part of the ship's life. Visitors might notice the odd hue of the oak in the passenger dining room. That came about from one of the famous practical jokes played onboard. *City of Milwaukee*'s captain, R.J. Martin, was an Irishman and proud of his heritage. Captain Martin preferred dining with the passengers rather than in the officer's dining room. He would frequently welcome passengers to the dining room himself. During one of the good captain's shore leaves, the crew painted the entire dining room shamrock green! Upon returning to the ship, Captain Martin went along with the joke for a while, but who could put up with a green dining room onboard a ship for very long? He ordered the culprits to strip the paint off his beloved hand rubbed oak paneling. Unfortunately, despite their best efforts, some green remained to tint the wood even today.

Captain Martin never did like the *City of Milwaukee*'s brass steam whistle, always complaining it sounded more like a duck than a ship's whistle. Once, while in a shipyard, he spotted a handsome steam whistle onboard another ship that was scheduled for dismantling. Captain Martin saw his opportunity. One night he invited the entire shipyard night shift to a local tavern for a drink that led to several more drinks. While the sly captain kept the workers busy, his crew was back at the shipyard making a switch. Nobody on shore had a

Highway History And Back Road Mystery

clue anything had happened until *City of Milwaukee* left port, when Captain Martin blew his brand new sweet sounding whistle, waving at the shipyard crowd as he sailed away with his stolen prize!

Perhaps the most memorable joke involving the *City of Milwaukee* was played on the Grand Trunk line's senior captain, Robert Cavanaugh, even before the ship was launched. Captain Cavanaugh can perhaps best be described as "difficult". He came by his nickname of Stormy Jack for good reason.

The *City of Milwaukee* was to be the flagship of the Grand Trunk

line, and as such would be Captain Cavanaugh's new command. The car ferries, though they boasted many amenities, offered less for senior officers than Captain Cavanaugh felt was appropriate. His personal pet peeve was the Captain's quarters, which featured a 3/4 size bed and shared a bathroom with other officers. One day Stormy Jack barged into the office of the company's purchasing agent and laid down the law. His new ship *would* feature private quarters appropriate for an officer of his stature. Captain Cavanaugh slammed his fist down on the poor man's desk and demanded a full size bunk, a private bathroom, and other appointments he felt were well deserved. The startled purchasing agent could only nod.

Well, the company had other ideas, and construction of the *City of Milwaukee* went right along according to schedule and as planned. But word had gotten out about Stormy Jack's tirade, and an elaborate prank was born. Workers at the shipyard began mentioning the extra work involved in building the Captain's quarters, always in his presence. Another Grand Trunk captain told Stormy Jack he had it on good authority the new ship was going to have imported Oriental rugs in the Captain's quarters. Shipyard workers talked about the exotic hardwoods to be used in the new ship's cabins. A very pleased Captain Cavanaugh heard passing conversations about his luxurious new private bathroom and huge bed. All the time, of course, nothing had changed.

Eventually the big day arrived and the *City of Milwaukee* was ready for her shakedown cruise. A huge crowd of shipyard workers, company officials, newspaper reporters, and guest passengers were on hand for the launching. Captain Cavanaugh strutted up the gangplank and made a beeline for his custom made new quarters, to the delight of everyone who was in on the joke.

The fusillade Stormy Jack unleashed that day is still talked about among Great Lakes sailors, and rivaled anything the wildest storm-swept lake could ever conjure up. Cursing everyone from the men who laid the ship's keel to the finish carpenters, Captain Cavanaugh marched right back down the gangplank and told company officials they could all go to hell, and that they could find someone else to command the new ship in the process! Captain Cavanaugh refused to set foot back aboard the *City of Milwaukee* for months, and another Grand Trunk captain, R.J. Martin commanded her during most of her working life. Eventually Stormy Jack did consent to take the ship out on a few occasions when Captain Martin was on leave, and ironically he died in his sleep aboard the *City of Milwaukee* in the 3/4 bed there in the very cabin that had so disappointed him.

A visit to the *City of Milwaukee* is a unique opportunity to experience a time in history that is rapidly fading from memory. Tours are held from May through October. Plans have been discussed to move the ship from Manistee to other Great Lakes ports during the winter to give people in places like Chicago and Cleveland an opportunity to experience life aboard a Great Lakes carferry. Preserving an old ship like the *City of Milwaukee* is an expensive proposition, and several ideas have been considered to raise revenues, including overnight lodging and dining aboard the ship. The ship is also available for private rental for receptions and other special events.

The *City of Milwaukee* is berthed at 51 Ninth Street in Manistee, Michigan. Touring the ship involves climbing up and down a series of ladders and stepping across high thresholds between passageways. The tour is not accessible for those in wheelchairs or unable to climb steep ladders. For more information on the *City of Milwaukee* call 231-398-0328, 231-882-7670, or log onto the Internet at www.carferry.com.

Christ Of The Ohio

Poised high on a hill overlooking the Ohio River in the tiny Indiana town of Troy stands a beautiful testament to love that was conceived during a terrible period of ugliness and hate.

The Christ of the Ohio monument towers nineteen feet tall, its arms outstretched in an eternal blessing to all who view it. The statue, visible to river traffic day and night thanks to floodlights that illuminate it after dark, was designed to be an inspiration to river travelers on their journey upriver. The story of the monument's creation is an often overlooked bit of history.

During World War II, a young German prisoner of war named Herbert Jogerst was in a prison camp in Kentucky, where he labored in a coal mine under harsh conditions. Years later Jogerst recalled the meager food available for the prisoners, the filthy clothing they lived in, and sleeping in a cold, damp cell. Every night prisoners were carried away to a hospital after succumbing to pneumonia. Many of the guards were as cruel as the living conditions the prisoners endured. Abuse at the hands of the guards or fellow prisoners was not uncommon.

Jogerst was an artist, a sculptor, and he had a strong faith in God. As he lay his head on the damp rag that served as his pillow every night, stretching his weary body on his cell's cold concrete floor, Jogerst prayed for deliverance. He promised God that if he managed to get out of the hell he was living in, he would someday find a way to show his appreciation. Jogerst remembered a priest, Father Paul, who occasionally visited the prison, and told the priest of his promise to God.

Maybe all of those prayers paid off, because eventually Jogerst was transferred to a prison camp in Indiana. After the war he was sent to England for eventual return to his home in Germany. One day, totally unexpectedly, Jogerst got a message from his old friend Father Paul, from his POW days. Father Paul told the artist of a wealthy doctor and his mother who lived high on a hill in Indiana, overlooking the Ohio River. The doctor and his mother wanted a work of art that would offer inspiration to travelers on the river. This was just the opportunity Herbert Jogerst needed to honor his promise to God during his days as a prisoner!

Returning to Indiana, Jogerst struggled for several years to come up with just the right material to endure the area's sometimes harsh climate, and something that would stand the test of time. Eventually he found just the right combination of terrazzatine dust and concrete and set to work creating his monument.

When finished, the statue was erected on a hill that once was owned by the Fulton family, one of whose sons, Robert, would go on to invent the steamboat. Since 1956 the Christ of the Ohio has been an Ohio River landmark. Herbert Jogerst's days as a prisoner of war may be long gone, but his testimonial to hope and salvation stands today, a reminder to all of us that even the worst of times will eventually pass and better days will surely follow.

Little Bighorn Battlefield

There were no real winners at the Battle of the Little Bighorn. Though the loss of Lieutenant Colonel George Armstrong Custer and 263 of his men at the hands of an overwhelming force of Plains Indians was a staggering defeat to the United States Army, ultimately the battle led to the final defeat of the Indian tribes and their confinement on reservations, ending centuries of free reign over their traditional homelands.

The clash of cultures that led up to Custer's fateful encounter with the hostile Indians on the rolling hills above the Little Bighorn River that hot June day in 1876 began years earlier as mountain men and fur trappers, followed by gold seeking prospectors and land hungry settlers, invaded the traditional homelands of the Lakota Sioux and Cheyenne. Understandably, the Plains tribes resisted, setting the stage for conflict, and the outcome was inevitable.

After years of hostilities with the Plains Indians, most notably the Lakota Sioux and Cheyenne, in 1868 the United States entered into the Treaty of Fort Laramie with the tribes, guaranteeing them a large portion of present-day eastern Wyoming as a permanent reservation. An uneasy peace lasted until 1874, when gold was discovered in the Black Hills, in the heart of the Indians' territory. Soon the gold rush was on, and prospectors swarmed into the area in search of the precious yellow metal.

At first the Army tried to keep the prospectors out of Indian lands, but it was impossible to stop the eager flood of fortune hunters. Next came efforts to buy the land from the Indians, who refused all overtures. The Lakota and Cheyenne left their reservations and began raiding, with the Army taking to the field in pursuit.

The 1876 campaign against the Indians consisted of three separate expeditions - one under Colonel John Gibbon, leaving from Fort Ellis in Montana Territory; one led by General Alfred H. Terry and setting out from Fort Abraham Lincoln in Dakota Territory; and the third leaving Fort Fetterman in Wyoming Territory under General George Crook. The Army's plan was to converge upon the Indians in their encampments in southeastern Montana Territory.

After their defeat at the Battle of the Rosebud River in mid-June, Crook's column was effectively out of the campaign and withdrew from the field. The Indians, relishing their victory, moved toward the Little Bighorn River. General Terry ordered Custer and his 7th Cavalry to enter the Little Bighorn from the south, traveling up the Rosebud River. Terry and his force, with Gibbon's column, then moved up the Yellowstone to come in from the north and trap the Indians.

At dawn on June 25, the 7th Cavalry located the Indian camp. Historians believe Custer, known for his bold and sometimes foolhardy aggressiveness, underestimated the Indians' strength, which is believed to have been several thousand. Dividing up his force of some 600 men, Custer ordered Captain Frederick W. Benteen to scout the bluffs to the south. Custer and Major Marcus A. Reno led the remainder of the force toward the Indian village. Splitting the column again, Custer took five companies of men and turned north, ordering Reno and his three companies to cross the river and attack. As Reno approached the spot where the Garryowen Post office is located today, he was attacked by a large force of warriors.

Reno tried to form a perimeter and fight back, but was forced to withdraw back across the river, where he set up a line of defense and was soon joined by Benteen. Heavy gunfire to the north told them that Custer and his troop were also heavily engaged. Moving northward about a mile to a spot now known as Weir Point, the soldiers made a stand and fought off a large force of Indians, holding their positions for nearly two days until the approach of reenforcements led by Terry and Gibbon drove the warriors off.

No one knows exactly what took place at Custer's battlefield, since no soldiers were left to tell the story. But historians have managed to re-create much of the battle based on artifacts and the location of the dead, as well as from interviews with Indians who fought there. Cheyenne Chief Two Moon later said that the warriors were like water swirling around a stone. "We shoot, we ride fast, we shoot again. Soldiers drop and horses fall on them." Custer and over 260 men were killed, the spots where many fell now marked with headstones. Reno and Benteen lost another 53 men. The Indians carried off their dead, but it is estimated that they lost no more than 100 men. After the battle, knowing that reprisals were sure, the tribes scattered and were eventually forced onto reservations.

Little Bighorn Battlefield National Monument, the site of Custer's defeat, lies in southeastern Montana in the Crow Indian Reservation, within a mile of Interstate 90. The monument is 65 miles from Billings, Montana and 70 miles north of Sheridan, Wyoming. Administered by the National Park Service, Little Bighorn National Monument is open daily. Vehicles pay a $6 entry fee. No overnight camping is allowed in the monument.

Besides the Custer Battlefield, the monument includes a National Cemetery where the dead from America's wars are buried, a visitor center that includes a museum with displays relating to the

Indian campaigns, and walking tours of the battlefield. A monument atop Last Stand Hill marks the mass grave of the soldiers who died in the battle. Park Rangers conduct several daily talks from Memorial Day through Labor Day, explaining various aspects of the Indian wars, life on the frontier (both from the Army and Indian point of view), and offering many details of the Battle of the Little Bighorn.

Walking along the paths of the monument, visitors can see headstones erected to mark the places where soldiers fell, and stop to let their minds wander back to that terrible day, when clouds of gun smoke shrouded the Little Bighorn and the hills echoed with the desperate cries of men in battle.

Historic Cove Fort

Frontier Utah was a wild and dangerous land in the mid-1800s. Hostile Indians, harsh weather, and the treacherous landscape made traveling hazardous and hampered the expansion of settlement. Mormon church leader Brigham Young knew that for his people to branch out into the southern regions of the territory, there must be some way to make covering the distance from more settled areas around Salt Lake to the new lands safer.

In 1860 a rancher named Charles Willden erected a ranch-fort at Cove Creek, near where present-day Interstates 15 and 70 meet in the southeast corner of Millard County, about twenty miles south of Kanosh. The site was midway between the communities of Fillmore and Beaver, a sixty mile journey that usually took two days. The small outpost, called Fort Willden, provided travelers some refuge in times of trouble, but was abandoned in 1865 during the Black Hawk War, leaving no safe haven in central Utah.

Recognizing a need for a permanent way station, Young chose Ira Hinckley to build a sturdy fort and to oversee the church ranch near the former site of Fort Willden. From April to November, 1867 a crew of volunteers quarried black volcanic rock and limestone and built Cove Fort.

The fort Ira Hinckley created was an impressive structure, with walls one hundred feet long, measuring eighteen feet high and up to four feet thick. The fort's wooden doors were filled with sand to stop bullets. There were twelve interior rooms serving the needs of the Hinckley family, the fort's personnel, and travelers passing through. Even a sustained attack would have little chance of breaching the fort's ramparts.

Fort Cove quickly became a popular stop with Mormon settlers, stagecoaches, freighters, and mail carriers. For years it was a busy place, with two daily stagecoaches making stops, traders and settlers passing through, and Pony Express riders switching horses. When Brigham Young made his frequent trips between Salt Lake City to St. George, Cove Fort was always a stopover. Always bustling with activity, Mrs. Hinckley would feed up to 75 people a day, while the blacksmith was kept busy repairing wagons and reshoeing horses and oxen. Cowboys tended to the church's tithing herd, while telegraph operators kept the wires humming with news.

Though there was never any serious Indian threat to Fort Cove, for over twenty years it was a bastion of church strength and provided safety for anyone passing through cental Utah, Mormon or not. As times changed and the area became more settled, the need for the fort disappeared, and eventually the church sold the property to a private owner about 1900.

For years the old fort was in private hands, and in 1989 the Hinckley family purchased the fort and donated it to the Mormon Church as a historic site. A five year restoration project followed, and in 1994 LDS Church President Gordon B. Hinckley, a grandson of Ira Hinckley, dedicated the Historic Fort Cove Complex.

Just as it was back in the days of the wild west, today Fort Cove is open to all travelers passing through central Utah who would like to get a glimpse of life in frontier times. Visitors can tour the fort's restored buildings and get a feeling of what it was like to experience life on the ragged edge of civilization. The Hinckley family living quarters, complete with period furnishings, look like the occupants just stepped outside to greet newcomers. Laundry hangs on a line in the washing room, a spinning wheel sits ready to go back to work, and the beds await at the end of a busy day.

The blacksmith shop has been carefully reconstructed, complete with a unique "oxen lift," a contraption that was designed to raise oxen off the ground to make shoeing them easier. In the bunkhouse, you can almost hear the heavy breathing of cowboys and freighters deep in sleep after their long day's labor. The telegraph room sits ready to receive news of the growing nation. Each room contains a fireplace to provide comfort against the harsh winter wind that blows through the old fort. You feel a connection with the old time pioneers as you walk in their footsteps through the fort's courtyards. Cove Fort makes a nice stop as you travel through the Beehive state, and provides a good look at one of the few pioneer fortifications still standing in good condition, out of the many built during territorial days.

Cove Fort is open daily from 8 a.m. to sunset, weather permitting. Admission is free and there is room to park RVs. The fort is located one mile north of Exit 1 off Interstate 70, and two miles south of Interstate 15.

Highway History And Back Road Mystery

History Lives At Colonial Michilimackinac

Long before the first French fur trader paddled his canoe through uncharted waters to discover the wonders of the Straits of Mackinac, Ottawa Indians knew the area well and came to trade with other tribes. For centuries the area was a meeting and trading area, and with the addition of the European influence, became even more important. In 1715, the French built a fort on the shore of Lake Michigan where Mackinaw City, Michigan is today, naming their outpost Fort Michilimackinac.

The French developed a good working relationship with the Indians, and Fort Michilimackinac became the hub of the North American fur trade. Merchants sent canoes laden with trade goods from the east to the fort, where their bales of blankets, beads, knives, hatchets, and other items prized on the frontier were bartered for pelts to feed the ever-hungry eastern and European markets. Fur traders, who spent the winter on the frontier living with the Indians, came to the fort to turn in the hides they had collected and load up with new trade goods before their return to the wilderness. Beaver was king, and the soft beaver pelts were in demand for the popular tri-cornered hats that were the fashion of the time. Many Frenchmen intermarried with local Indians and a small settlement of merchants, traders, and other non-military personnel grew up at the fort. Today, the French influence can still be seen throughout the region in the names of cities, landmarks, and streets.

As the British pressed westward from their foothold along the eastern coast, a clash with their traditional French enemies was inevitable, and a series of hostilities over many years came to be known as the French and Indian Wars as the two world powers struggled for control of the area and the rich fur trade. Though Fort Michilimackinac never came under fire during these outbreaks of violence, troops from the fort and their Indian allies ventured out to raid settlements as far away as New York, Indiana, and Ohio.

In 1761 the defeated French relinquished control of Fort Michilimackinac, and the British seized control of much of the New World, as well as the fur business. The British quickly proved themselves to be unschooled in the ways of the frontier. They refused to send traders out to meet and barter with the Indians, insisting instead that the tribes come to them. They reduced the amount they would give the Indians for their furs, did not associate socially with the tribes, and acted imperiously toward the native peoples.

This arrogance may have served the British well in their more civilized colonies, but it was a dangerous practice on the frontier, and quickly strained relationships with the Indians. Things came to a head on June 2, 1763. A band of Chippewa Indians were playing a game similar to modern-day lacrosse, and their ball went over the fort's wall. Several Indians ran inside the fort, under the ruse of retrieving the ball. Once inside, they pulled hatchets from under their clothing and attacked the surprised garrison. Most of the British troops were killed, the survivors taken captive. The attack was part of a larger uprising across the frontier led by Chief Pontiac, and the chastened British learned their lesson. After things settled down a year later, the British treated the Indians far better, and eventually a strong alliance developed between the two cultures.

During the American Revolution, the British feared rebels would attack their outpost, and moved to Mackinac Island, where they established Fort Mackinac. Fort Michilimackinac was disassembled and moved across the water to the island, and what couldn't be moved was burnt to the ground to prevent it from falling into American hands. The wilderness soon reclaimed Fort Michilimackinac.

Today the old fur trading outpost has been rebuilt on its original ruins, and Colonial Michilimackinac offers visitors a chance to experience life in a 1770s frontier outpost. Here you can watch red coated soldiers drill, traditionally costumed fur traders barter for goods, a frontier woman scrubbing clothes by hand, take part in a colonial wedding, and watch archaeologists uncover artifacts from the fort's past.

Less than a mile from downtown Mackinaw City, when you walk thorough the fort's gates you step back over 200 years in time. This is a living history experience, and it isn't hard to let your mind transport you back to the days when colorful fur traders, called voyageurs, arrived with their goods, when Indians gathered outside the stockade's walls to barter their furs, and the events that shaped our nation's future were daily events.

The soldiers' barracks, traders' cabins, officers' quarters, trading post, church, and other buildings have all been reconstructed with exact attention to detail. Step inside the commanding officer's quarters and see how he lived in relative comfort, then go into the troops' communal barracks and marvel at the differences. Imagine what it was like to sleep two to a bed for warmth during winter, to live for months at a time on a diet of salt pork and beans, and to suffer the harsh punishments meted out for infractions of the rules.

At the trading post, piles of supplies are displayed, waiting to temp the fur traders and Indians out of their pelts. One of the most successful fur traders was Ezekiel Solomon, Michigan's first Jewish

Highway History And Back Road Mystery

settler. A native of Germany, Solomon served in the British army, and arrived with the British contingent that replaced the French in 1761. Solomon, who was known for treating the Indians fairly, was one of the few to escape death at the hands of the Indians during Pontiac's Uprising in 1763. His cabin has been rebuilt in the fort and is a look at the life of a prosperous merchant on the frontier.

Throughout the day, scheduled events at Colonial Michilimackinac give visitors a first hand view of life on the frontier, as costumed guides fire muskets, cook over fireplaces, and tend to livestock. A washerwoman demonstrates the perils of a "knuckle buster" washboard to visitors, while a short distance away, a uniformed British solider plays music for children on a jaw harp, and everyone is invited to attend a frontier wedding ceremony. After the bride and groom are pronounced man and wife, everyone files out-

side to join in the dancing and celebrating.

Visitors can enhance their experience to Colonial Michilimackinac with the opportunity to participate in many of the fort's events; taking part in the Arrival of the Voyageurs as traders arrive with loads of goods, learning how to cook over an open fire, or tending a garden. Be careful, the army recruiter is always looking for new troops, and before you know it, this smooth talking redcoat may have you serving the King in some remote outpost!

One of the most popular events at the fort is the firing of the cannon. Visitors file out the lakeside gate and gather around as a salute is fired over the water with a great burst of smoke and fire. One has to wonder what it must be like to be passing by in a modern day Great Lakes freighter and spy a frontier fort flying the British flag firing on you with a centuries old cannon.

Since the 1950s, archaeologists have been actively working at the old fort, painstakingly uncovering and cataloging artifacts that include old trade beads, weapons, crockery, belt buckles, and other leftovers from the past. Many of these items are on display, and others are being discovered every day. Visitors can watch as tiny artifacts are unearthed, gently sifted through screens, and carefully brushed clean.

In one of the buildings, a flight of stairs lead down to the original foundations, where the efforts to discover the secrets of the past are explained. Scientists have been able to clearly define the three periods of human activity - Indian, French, and British - at Fort Michilimackinac by studying the strata layers containing artifacts from each occupation. It is amazing to see how well preserved many of the artifacts are after their centuries underground.

When the British abandoned the fort, they burned the old powder magazine to prevent it from falling into Rebel hands. Ironically, the fire did much to preserve the structure's history for future excavation. When the roof fell in, it extinguished the flames, and covered musket balls and other artifacts, as well as the building's timbers, protecting them until modern-day archaeologists could unearth them. Visitors can go down a short flight of steps to see the original foundation of the power magazine.

Colonial Michilimackinac, with its period-costumed guides, its old buildings, and its demonstrations of frontier life and skills, is an interesting and fun look back into time. As you stroll past the watchtowers, among the cottages, and past the gardens, it is hard to remember that there is a world of televisions, automobiles, and grocery stores waiting just outside the fort's walls.

Colonial Michilimackinac is open daily from early May through mid-October. One very popular event at the fort is the annual Fort Michilimackinac Historical Reenactment Pageant, held on Memorial Day weekend, when some 400 local residents and history fans don the authentic dress of the fort's colonial days and take part in a re-enactment of the fort's history, including the Indian uprising in 1761.

The Visitor Center at Colonial Michilimackinac has a nice selection of souvenirs and local history books, and is your gateway to the fort.

There is so much to see and do in Mackinaw City and the surrounding area that you could never do it in less than a week, so take advantage of the town's hospitality and get to know Colonial Michilimackinac and everything else the region has to offer.

Dade Battlefield

The story of early American expansion in Florida was written in blood. For years whites and Seminole Indians had clashed in quick, violent confrontations over land, cattle and slaves. These ongoing conflicts helped justify the United States government's policy of removing native peoples to reservations far away from their homelands. Washington decreed that all Seminoles be removed to reservations in Oklahoma starting on January 1, 1836.

Well aware that the Indians would strongly resist being deposed, military authorities began strengthening the small garrison at Fort King, in what is present-day Ocala, where the government had set up an Indian agency to oversee the removal of the Seminoles. In late December, 1835 Major Francis L. Dade was picked to lead a relief column from Fort Brooke, at present-day Tampa. The Seminole had other plans. The Second Seminole War was about to begin.

Osceola, the great chief of the Seminoles, planned to kill Wiley Thompson, the Indian agent at Fort King, then join chiefs Alligator and Miscanopy to ambush Dade's column of infantry and artillery troops.

The route along the Fort King Military Road was a harsh trek, made even worse by the weather. For five days the soldiers battled rain, cold and rough terrain as they made their way north, unaware that the Indians were watching them every step of the way from the edges of the thick forest along the trail.

On the morning of December 28, Major Dade assembled his 107 cold and weary troops and tried to lift their spirits, promising that with two-thirds of their trip behind them, including the most dangerous ambush sites, the end was near. "Our difficulties and dangers are over now," Dade told his men, and promised them three days of rest and a belated Christmas celebration once they reached

Fort King. Dade and his men had no idea they had only moments left to live.

About 8 a.m. the troop column was making its way through open terrain in a cold rain. The wet and miserable men trudged along, their coats draped over their muskets and ammunition boxes to protect them. Complacent now that he felt they were in safe territory, Major Dade failed to send out his scouts to guard their flanks, an error that would prove disastrous. Hidden under cover of pines and palmettos, 180 Seminoles waited for the signal to fire.

The Indians' first volley was fired at close range and tore through the military column, killing or wounding half of the soldiers. Among the first killed were Major Dade and Captain Upton S. Fraser. Three of the six officers who survived that first attack were wounded.

Captain George W. Gardiner managed to rally the panicked soldiers still standing and returned fire with a six-pound cannon, driving the Indians back a short distance and allowing the soldiers time to throw up a hasty breastwork of logs and brush. While some of the troops tended to the wounded, Captain Gardiner ordered others to collect ammunition and weapons from the bodies of the dead.

Soon the Seminoles rallied and launched a second attack that continued unabated until about 2 p.m. By then there was no return fire from the low breastwork. Most of Major Dade's command was dead. The Seminoles and their allies, a collection of runaway slaves, swarmed over the few surviving troops. Hatchets and knives flashed and were soon stained crimson. Three wounded soldiers, Joseph Sprague, Ransom Clarke, and Edwin DeCourey somehow were left for dead and managed to escape. DeCourey died soon after, but Clarke and Sprague managed to make it back to Fort Brooke alive. Major Dade's black interpreter, Louis Pacheco was spared and taken captive.

The ambush was a success for the Seminoles, who had only three warriors killed and five wounded. After looting the soldiers' bodies and dumping the column's cannon into a nearby pond, they withdrew to Wahoo Swamp to celebrate their victory.

Seven weeks later, on February 20, 1836, General Edmund P.

Highway History And Back Road Mystery

Gaines led an expedition to the ambush site. The bodies of the slain troops were identified and given proper military burials. The eight fallen officers were interred on the east side of the trail, and the 98 enlisted men were buried in two mass graves within the log breastwork that had been their final stand. The column's cannon was retrieved from the pond where the Indians had dumped it and mounted muzzle down at the head of the officers' graves as a monument to the fallen troops. Six years later, on August 14, 1842, the men of Dade's command were laid to rest in the National Cemetery in St. Augustine. The expenses involved in moving the bodies were met by donations from other soldiers and officers.

While the Seminoles won the battle, their days were doomed and eventually most of the tribe was forced onto reservations the government had set up in Oklahoma, a land totally unsuited to their traditional way of life.

Today the ambush site is Dade Battlefield Historic State Park and is located in Bushnell, Florida, five or six miles off of Interstate 75. Every year re-enactments of the battle are held under the huge live oaks and pine flats where the brave men of Major Dade's column perished. The park includes a visitor center with exhibits and artifacts from the Seminole Wars, a re-creation of the log breastwork the soldiers used for defense, a bandstand, playground, and picnic area with restrooms. An interpretive trail meanders through the forest where the battle raged. Trail labels mark the military road and battlefield. Well behaved pets are allowed in the park, but must be kept on a leash at all times.

The park is a quiet, peaceful place that belies the terrible suffering that went on here. Today children frolic and squirrels play where once men were engaged in deadly battle, one side fighting to preserve the only way of life they had ever known, the other fighting in vain just to survive.

Dade Battlefield Historic State Park is open daily from 8 a.m. until sunset. For more information, write Dade Battlefield Historic State Park, 7200 C.R. 603 South Battlefield Drive, Bushnell, Florida 33513, or call 352-793-4781.

Ethan Allen
Vermont's Revolutionary War Hero

Ethan Allen wore many titles in his life. Flamboyant frontiersman. Courageous and daring military leader. Outlaw. Land speculator. Suspected traitor. Prisoner of war. Hero. He was all of these and much more.

Born in Litchfield, Connecticut on January 10, 1738, Allen was the oldest of eight children born to Joseph and Mary Allen. When his father died at an early age, the responsibility to provide for the large family fell on Ethan's shoulders. He took on this duty without complaint and worked hard to help raise his younger siblings. In 1764 he married Mary Brownson and in 1769 he moved to the region known as the New Hampshire Land Grant (in what is present day Vermont), settling in Bennington. Both New York and New Hampshire were vying for control of the region, and Ethan soon found himself involved in the debate.

The governor of New York had levied taxes and sold land grants in the area on parcels that were already claimed by the original settlers, causing unrest and anger on the frontier. In 1770 the New York Supreme Court declared all of the New Hampshire land grants and claims invalid, a decision that would require the settlers to buy their own land back from New York or risk losing their homes.

By this time Allen had fought in the French and Indian War, and he helped raise a militia, calling themselves the Green Mountain Boys, after the Green Mountains of Vermont. The band was essentially vigilantes who used intimidation, threats, and violence to protect the land from New Yorkers and drive out surveyors sent by the New York governor. Ethan Allen was appointed a colonel for the Green Mountain Boys. Soon after, New York's governor declared him an outlaw and put a price on his head. Catching the wily frontiersman was no easy task, and Allen eluded capture and continued to lead the Green Mountain Boys in their struggle.

When the Revolutionary War broke out, the Green Mountain Boys sided with the patriots attempting to overthrow British rule. The colonists had their first major victory of the war on May 10, 1775 when Allen, Colonel Benedict Arnold (who later turned traitor and whose name is now synonymous with turncoat), and 83 Green Mountain Boys captured Fort Ticonderoga, a strategic outpost that was well armed. The weapons taken from the fort were well used in patriot hands, and the emotional impact of their victory was felt on both sides of the conflict, greatly boosting the colonists' morale while shaking the confidence of the British.

The victory pales a bit when one learns that Fort Ticonderoga was taken without a struggle. The British stationed there probably did not even know the war had started yet. Allen's band basically overpowered a couple of guards, and he knocked on the commander's door in the middle of the night and demanded his surrender in "the name of the Great Jehovah and the Continental Congress." At least that is how history quotes Ethan Allen during the encounter. Israel Harris, one of the Green Mountain Boys who witnessed the event later claimed Allen really banged on the door of the officer's cabin and yelled "Come out of there you damned old rat!" Whatever he may have said, it worked and Ethan Allen was an instant hero. George Washington said of Ethan Allen "There is an original something about him that commands inspiration." Benedict Arnold, by then a general and unimpressed with Allen's band of roughnecks, was not so flattering, being quoted as saying "He is a proper man to head his own band of wild people, but entirely unacquainted with military service."

Not one to rest on his laurels, Allen decided if he could do it once, he could do it again. The Green Mountain Boys next captured the British fort at Crown Point. Heady with his success, he launched a badly planned, badly executed raid on Montreal. Many of the Green Mountain Boys realized the folly of this latest maneuver and refused to participate. The British there were not so ill prepared, and Ethan Allen was captured and imprisoned on the schooner *Gaspe* and transported to England. He was a popular prisoner and spent the rest of the war entertaining his British captors with stories of life on the wild frontier. Some claimed that this fraternization was an act of treason, but Allen, always an opportunist, simply saw it as making the most of a bad situation.

With the American victory in the war, Ethan Allen returned to Vermont and settled in Burlington. He and his brother Ira bought up several tracts of land and Allen built a homestead on the Winooski (Onion) River.

Allen became a successful farmer and trader, and he achieved a very nice lifestyle. The basement of his home was always well stocked with goods he had acquired in his trading ventures north into Canada. He campaigned hard for statehood for Vermont, a goal he would not live to see happen.

Allen lived on his homestead until 1789. He became ill while returning from a trading trip and died on February 12, at the age of 52. Local history says that Allen, a man who enjoyed his drink, imbibed a bit too much and fell down while crossing the frozen surface of Lake Champlain, coming down with a case of pneumonia. Two years after his death Vermont would achieve statehood.

Over the years Ethan Allen's homestead passed through several hands, and for many years the Pease Grain Company owned the land and a manager lived in the old house Ethan Allen built. By the late 1970s the home's history had been forgotten and the land was under contract to a developer who planned to demolish the old house. Noted Vermont historian and scholar Ralph Nading Hill stepped into the picture and launched an effort to save the historic homestead. At first, many considered Hill a kook, but his research soon proved his claim that this had indeed been Ethan Allen's home. Wealthy friends and supporters of Hill's helped establish the Ethan Allen Homestead Trust to restore and preserve the old warrior's home.

Over the years the homestead has been carefully restored using many period items to make it as correct as possible to Ethan Allen's era. Visitors to the homestead can tour the house and surrounding land with guides well versed in the history of the site. The tour begins with a fourteen minute multimedia presentation in a replica of a 1700s tavern, telling the story of Ethan Allen and the Green Mountain Boys. From there, guides lead the way down a path through beautiful old black locust trees to the two story home where Allen and his family lived until his death.

The house is furnished as it would have been when Ethan Allen lived here, and during certain times volunteers in period costume actually cook on the old kitchen fireplace, giving visitors a memorable experience back in time. Artifacts found during excavations at the homestead are on display in the house and visitors center. Many are believed to have been used by the Allen family during their stay at the homestead. The homestead occupies rolling fields and scenic curves along the river bank, and includes the house and historic gardens the Allen family used.

Kitchen gardens provided both food and herbs for early day settlers. Culinary herbs were used for seasoning, while medicinal herbs were employed as remedies for the sick or injured. Fanny's Garden (named after Ethan Allen's second wife) at the homestead is planted with heirloom vegetables and herbs that were used during frontier times, including parsnip, flax, witch hazel, anise, coriander, and pennyroyal. One vegetable not found in the garden are tomatoes. In the eighteenth century, tomatoes were considered poisonous.

A visit to the Ethan Allen Homestead is an opportunity to get a closer look at colonial life and to get better acquainted with the unique character who is Vermont's favorite hero. The homestead is located just north of Burlington and is open from mid-May to mid-October. For more information on the Ethan Allen Homestead, call (802)-865-4556 or visit their website at www.sover.net/~eahome.

Fort Caroline

European foothold in the New World

In the mid-16th century, mortal enemies Spain and France were engaged in a frenzy of empire-building. France, emerging from feudalism, dreamed of the glories to be had as a world power. Spain, already the world's strongest nation, had gained a solid foothold in the Americas and had established sea lanes throughout the Caribbean. Heavily loaded with gold and silver, Spanish ships carried their treasures back to Europe on a regular schedule. France wanted a share of the riches Spain was gathering through trade and plunder and jealously guarded.

France's first attempt to stake a claim in North America was at La Caroline, a settlement near the mouth of Florida's St. Johns River, at present day Jacksonville. The original plan was for a commercial venture at La Caroline, but conflicts in France expanded the plan. Faced with growing religious persecution, Admiral Gaspard de Coligny, the most powerful leader of the Huguenots, (French Protestants), suggested to the monarchy that the New World colony also be a refuge for his people.

Jean Ribault led an exploratory expedition to North America in February, 1562. Landing at the mouth of the May River (now the St. Johns), Ribault erected a monument to establish France's claim to the area, then sailed north, leaving a small garrison at Charlesfort, near Port Royal Sound, before sailing back home. Short on supplies and woodcraft skills, within a very short time conditions became desperate, and Ribault's men returned to France.

A persistent Admiral Coligny urged the crown to make another attempt at colonization, and in April, 1564, Rene de Goulaine de Laudonniere lead some 200 soldiers and craftsmen on a voyage back to the May River. Landing in June, the colonists started to build a village and fort on the river's south bank. They named their settlement La Caroline (land of Charles), after French King Charles IX.

Relations with the local Timucuan Indians, originally good, had soured by the following spring, and without their support the colonists were close to starvation. There were reports that some colonists had resorted to cannibalism to survive. Internal strife led a group to leave La Caroline, hoping to make their way back home. They were instead captured by the Spanish, and revealed the location of the interloping settlement. The remaining French colonists were in desperate straits when Ribault arrived in August, 1565 with a relief expedition of supplies, along with 600 soldiers and settlers, including several women and children.

On learning of the growing French incursion in Florida, Spain's King Philip II sent a force led by Admiral Pedro Menendez to eject the colonists. Hoping to wait until Ribault returned to Europe, Menendez established a base at St. Augustin, to the south, and prepared to evict the French with force, if necessary. Ribault, wanting to strike the first blow, sailed south to attack the Spanish, but a hurricane destroyed his fleet, scattering the ships and beaching them far to the south.

Quick to take advantage of the opportunity, Menendez marched north with 500 soldiers to attack the lightly guarded French settlement. Early on the morning of September 20, 1565, the Spaniards swooped down on La Caroline, massacring 140 settlers. Only 60 women and children were spared and taken prisoner. A handful of colonists, including Laudonniere, escaped and sailed back to France.

Leaving a small force to occupy the fort, Menendez next led his soldiers south, where they found the survivors of the shipwrecked French fleet, including their admiral, Ribault. Throwing themselves on his mercy, the Frenchmen begged Menendez for their lives. But it wasn't a time for mercy. At a place later named Matanzas (slaughter), 350 of the survivors were put to the sword. Menendez spared only a few, who claimed to be Catholics.

The French took their revenge in April, 1568, when they attacked and burned La Caroline, killing any Spaniard that did not escape.

The Spanish rebuilt the fort, but abandoned it a year later. France never again strongly challenged Spanish claims to North America.

Today the site of La Caroline is a National Memorial, administered by the National Parks Service. A replica of the fort has been

built at the mouth of the St. Johns River, where visitors can stand on the banks and look across the river, alive today with traffic. The Visitor Center has displays on the fort's history, the culture of the Timucuan people, and the local geology. Nearby, at the mouth of the river, stands a re-creation of the monument Ribualt erected to stake France's claim in 1562. Fort Caroline is a unit of the Timucuan Ecological and Historical Preserve. The park is located thirteen miles east of downtown Jacksonville, off Atlantic Boulevard. Fort Caroline is open daily, and there is no admission charge.

Highway History And Back Road Mystery

Pioneer Grave

In a tiny roadside park sandwiched between U.S. Highway 26 and the Burlington Northern railroad tracks on the eastern edge of Scotts Bluff, Nebraska sits the lonely grave of Rebecca Winters, one of the thousands of pioneers who set out in search of a better life in the west and never made it. But unlike so many of her fellow travelers who succumbed to disease, injury, and Indian attack on the westward trek and were buried in unmarked graves, Rebecca Winters' final resting place is commemorated with a metal historical marker and a gravestone in tribute to the respect she earned from her family and fellow pioneers. Her story is a prime example of the hardships and perils that faced the early settlers making their way westward.

Rebecca Winters was born in New York state in 1802, the daughter of Gideon Burdick, who had fought in the Revolutionary War.

Rebecca, a very warm and caring person, and her husband Hiram were among the earliest members of the Mormon Church, being baptized into the faith in June of 1833. In those days of intolerance, Mormons often faced severe persecution at the hands of non-believers, and the Winters family was no exception. They were forced to relocate several times, seeking new homes in Ohio, Illinois, and Iowa. Finally, in June of 1852, the family joined with other members of the Mormon Church to make the trip west to Utah, part of the great exodus to the new land where they hoped they could live in peace.

The frontier held many perils for the hapless immigrants making their way west. Flooded rivers could sweep a wagon away and pull its occupants under. Bears, wolves, and rattlesnakes sometimes lay in wait of the careless trespasser, and there was always the threat of marauding Indians. But the biggest danger was cholera. The dreaded disease killed thousands during the course of the westward migration. Somewhere along the Platte Valley, several people in the Winters' wagon train contracted the disease, among them Rebecca. She died on August 15, 1852.

Usually when an emigrant died, their graves were hidden by their family. often dug directly in the roadway, and wagons were driven over the grave to destroy all signs of its presence. This may seem callous to us, but there was a practical reason for the practice, it reduced the chances of wild animals finding and disturbing the grave. There was seldom time, or even in materials, to erect any sort of grave marker.

Rebecca Winters was a rare exception. Her husband and a close family friend, William Reynolds. went to great lengths to preserve her grave, a testament to how well she was loved by all who knew her. They dug an unusually deep grave, then lined the bottom with a layer of planks from abandoned wagons. Rebecca's friends and family couldn't bear the thought of dirt touching her, so her body was carefully wrapped in blankets and a second layer of planks was placed over it. After the grave was filled in, William Reynolds chiseled the words "Rebecca Winters, Age 50" into a metal wagon rim. Reynolds' daughter Ellis held a candle for him to see by as he worked into the night. The rim was bent into an oval approximating the outline of a tombstone and embedded over Rebecca's grave. Their sad chore done, the family and their companions continued on their journey west, finally settling in Pleasant Grove, Utah.

The crude grave marker that William Reynolds fashioned stood through decades of prairie winters, fierce summer storms, and wildfires, and in 1899 it led to the rediscovery of the grave by a team of surveyors planning a route for the Burlington Northern railroad. The tale goes that, out of respect for the grave, the railroad's original route was changed slightly to protect it, and the tracks were laid a few feet from the grave.

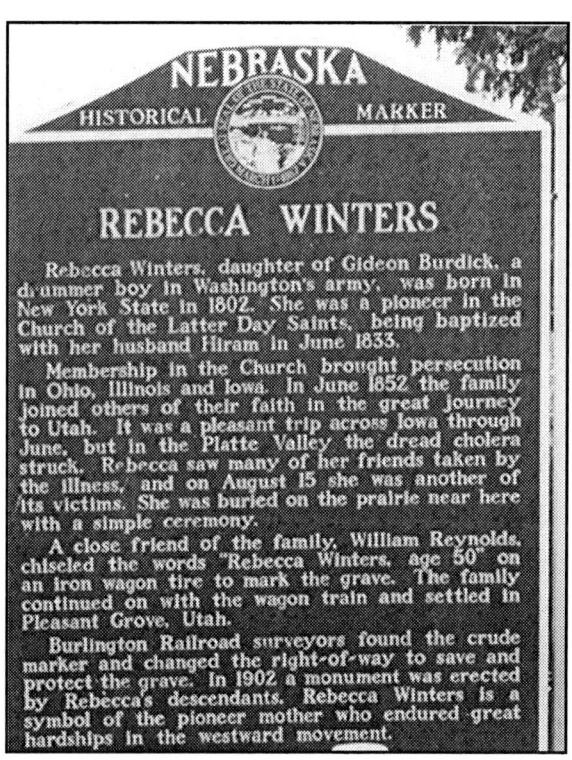

At the end of the twentieth century, expanding rail traffic and an increasing number of visitors to the grave site raised concerns for visitor safety, and the railroad contacted the Winters family descendants for permission to move the grave to a safer, more accessible location. The family agreed, and on September 5, 1995 a team of archaeologists from the Nebraska State Historical Society opened the grave, with 65 members of the Winters family looking on.

Highway History And Back Road Mystery

Rebecca's remains, were removed to a new site only 400 yards away, just off Highway 26, where she was again laid to rest in a beautiful mahogany casket on October 14, 1995. Some 125 of Rebecca's descendants were on hand for the solemn ceremony, including her 16 year old great-great-great-granddaughter, also named Rebecca Winters. Also attending the service was the great- granddaughter of William Reynolds, the man who had chiseled the metal marker at the original burial, 143 years before. Today the wagon rim still stands over the grave as it has for nearly a century and a half. a tribute to a much loved pioneer woman and the respect in which she was held by those who knew her.

Fort Meigs
Bastion of the War of 1812

Today the scene high atop a bluff overlooking the Maumee River in northwestern Ohio is serene. Canoes navigate the water below, squirrels scamper along the limbs of ancient trees, while birds flit from branch to branch. It's hard to relate this quiet setting to the pivotal battles fought here, but nearly 200 years ago, Fort Meigs became the focal point in the War of 1812.

Until the spring of 1813, the war in the Northwest had gone badly for the Americans. Between June of 1812 and February, 1813, the United States lost both Fort Mackinac and Detroit, in Michigan Territory, as well as Fort Dearborn in Illinois Territory, and American forces were defeated in battle on the Raisin River in Michigan. Only Fort Wayne, in Indiana Territory, withstood British attack.

Determined to make a stand in Ohio, the commander of the Northwest Army, General William Henry Harrison, established a fort on the south side of the Maumee River on February 2, 1813. The new post was intended to serve as a temporary supply depot and staging area for an invasion of Canada.

Named for Ohio Governor Return Jonathan Meigs, the earth and wood palisade enclosed nearly ten acres and boasted seven two-story blockhouses, five artillery batteries, two underground powder magazines, and various work and storage buildings. Troop strength ranged from less than 900 to over 2,000 and compromised Regulars, militia from Ohio, Kentucky, Pennsylvania, and Virginia, and several companies of independent volunteers. Because the fort was more an armed camp than a formally engineered fortification, most troops lived in tents inside the stockade.

Life could be demanding at the frontier outpost, and many soldiers died from illness and disease. Troops received a meager ration,

Highway History And Back Road Mystery

which they were expected to supplement by hunting, fishing, and growing gardens. Discipline was harsh, with punishment for infractions of rules ranging from extra duty to lashings. For those injured or wounded in battle, the crude medical and surgical procedures available were often worse than the injury.

The British laid siege to Fort Meigs on May 1, 1813. General Harrison, with 1,200 defenders and nearly thirty pieces of artillery under his command, was confident that he could withstand the assault, if his small supply of ammunition held out. Harrison knew that reinforcements were on the way, and used his artillery batteries sparingly, rewarding any soldier who retrieved a British cannonball to use in return fire with a gig of whisky.

The bombardment lasted four days before the reinforcement troop of Kentucky militiamen arrived on the scene. Some of the Kentucky reinforcements were captured and later killed by English-allied Indians. The siege lasted another five days before the British withdrew, giving the Americans a significant victory in the Northwest and turning the tide of the war.

While the British saw the withdrawal from Fort Meigs as a prudent maneuver, their Indian allies were bitterly disappointed and the King's troops feared losing their support. To appease them, the British once again attacked Fort Meigs in July.

Indians staged a mock battle to lure the fort's garrison outside the walls under the illusion that a relief column was under attack, but the Americans didn't fall for the ruse. Heartened by their earlier victory, once again the defenders withstood the siege.

Finally giving up, the British moved on to Fort Stevens, where they also failed to defeat the Americans, and suffered heavy losses, forcing their retreat into Canada. On September 10, 1813 Commodore Oliver Hazard Perry defeated the British fleet on Lake Erie, and the United states finally had the upper hand in the Northwest.

The threat eliminated, General Harrison transferred all but 100 men from Fort Meigs and ordered the fort dismantled. In its place, a small stockade was built to serve as a supply base and to protect the rapids of the Maumee River. In December, 1814 Harrison was victorious in the Battle of Thames and fighting in the Northwest was over. A peace treaty was signed in May, 1814, and a year later American troops formally abandoned Fort Meigs.

Over the next 150 years the Maumee River area became heavily populated, early settlers giving way to larger farms, and those in turn giving way to small towns and suburbs. The old fort site lay under farmland until 1965, when the Ohio Historical Society began to reconstruct the stockade as it was during the British siege of 1813. The project was completed in 1975, and officially dedicated in 1976.

Today the old fort looks much as it did during it's proud past, with the seven blockhouses sporting walls two feet thick and four inch deep window and cannon port shutters. Several of the blockhouses feature exhibits and dioramas of the War of 1812, the fort's construction and reconstruction of Fort Meigs, and the lives of the soldiers who garrisoned the fort.

Visitors can climb to the second floor gun ports and look out over the battleground from where defenders took aim at the enemy. On the Grand Battery, you can stand where General Harrison did as he watched in frustration and horror as members of the Kentucky militia were trapped and taken prisoner across the river. On the Grand Parade, you can imagine soldiers receiving the General Orders of the day, drawing their whiskey ration, or witnessing the punishment of their fellow soldiers who disobeyed regulations. A handsome monument towering over the middle of the fort honors the gallant men who served here.

A stone house, built by the Works progress Administration in the 1930s, houses a visitor center where you can purchase souvenirs and a very nice collection of books. The parks grounds are open for picnicking during daylight hours. During good weather, the fort holds re-enactments of Revolutionary War encampments and battles, as well as fife and drum concerts and demonstrations of cannon and musket firing.

Fort Meigs is located a few miles west of Toledo, Ohio and is open April through October from 9:30 a.m. to 5 p.m. Wednesday through Saturday, and noon to 5 p.m. Sundays and holidays. For information about events at Fort Meigs, call 1-800-BUCKEYE.

A Stolen Shrine?

In St. Augustine Church, located in the tiny southern Indiana community of Leopold, is displayed a shrine with a unique history. Its story is one of love and redemption that grew out of a time of sorrow and despair.

In the darkest days of the Civil War, three Union soldiers from Perry County, Indiana were captured during the battle of Chimauga and interred in the notorious Confederate prison at Andersonville, Georgia. Andersonville was a hell hole of misery and suffering, overcrowded and with no facilities to handle the thousands of prisoners who were held there. Food and water were in short supply, while disease and starvation were everywhere.

During the fourteen months the prison was operating, more than 45,000 Union soldiers were confined at Andersonville. Of those, almost 13,000 died from disease, malnutrition, poor sanitation, overcrowding, and exposure to the elements. To bring that number into more understandable terms, that is a rate of over 30 men a day, every day for fourteen months. One death every 48 minutes, 24 hours a day, seven days a week.

The three Perry County prisoners of war, Lambert Rogier, Henry Devillez, and Isidore Naviaux were thrown into this pit of suffering and tried as best they could to stay alive. Strength was in numbers, and their bond of friendship helped them to endure their hardships and suffering. Their strong religious faith also played an important role in their survival. Every day they prayed for deliverance, and promised themselves that if they survived, they would build a shrine in their church back home to show their gratitude.

Whether it was Divine Intervention or their strong willpower, all three men managed to stay alive and were freed at the war's end. Returning home to Indiana, they did not forget their promise made back in Andersonville.

Henry Devillez came from Belgium as a boy of fourteen, and he remembered the lovely Shrine of Our Lady of Consolation in the Duchy of Luxembourg. In their darkest days in prison, he had told his two companions about the shrine, and they decided it was the perfect tribute of their respect and gratitude.

The shrine had a long and interesting history. In 1628 a small chapel was being built near the city of Luxembourg when disaster struck. The plague hit the region, taking thousands of lives. The death toll was so high that cemeteries of the time could not hold all of the dead and their bodies were burned in mass fires.

Father Broquart, the priest in charge of building the chapel, was one of those struck down by the disease. Laying in his bed, feverish and near death, he prayed for the strength to recover and complete his task. He vowed that if he was allowed to finish the construction, he would dedicate the chapel to Mary, Consoler of the Afflicted.

Almost overnight the priest's fever fell and he was soon back on his feet and back at work. True to his word, when the chapel was completed it was dedicated to Our Lady of Consolation, and a statue of the Blessed Mother holding the baby Jesus was placed on the altar. The statue is a work of art. Both figures are dressed in white, with blue capes trimmed in gold, and each wears a jeweled crown. Mary holds a gold scepter and a silver heart is suspended from her arm. Jesus holds a silver ball and cross. People flocked to the chapel to pray for cures from many illnesses and diseases, and the faithful believed many of those prayers were answered. Several of these cures are recognized as bona fide miracles by the Catholic Church.

Lambert Rogier traveled to Belgium to have an exact duplicate of the shrine made. The official story says he was successful in his quest, and brought the duplicate of the icon back to St. Augustine Church, where it was placed on display.

Or did he?

There is another story. Some say that Rogier was not able to find an artist capable of recreating the statue's beauty, and that finally, in frustration, he stole the original and brought it back to Indiana. Some historians claim the theft sparked an international incident between the United States and Belgium. According to their version of the tale, things got pretty hot until Belgium's King Leopold was told that Leopold, Indiana, where the statue was taken to, was named in his honor. So delighted was King Leopold that he relented and allowed the statue to remain at St. Augustine Church, where it remains displayed prominently today.

So which story is true? Did three prisoners of war dedicate a copy of the holy relic to their church, or is the real statue from Belgium on display in this small community tucked away on a back road in Indiana?

Highway History And Back Road Mystery

George Washington Carver
From slave to scientist

His beginnings were humble. He was born a slave near the end of the Civil War on a small Missouri farm. By the age of 55, he had risen to national prominence as a scientist, educator, botanist, agronomist, artist and "cookstove chemist." George Washington Carver's achievements were legendary, and for many he was a role model who set standards for others to achieve. Yet, throughout his life Carver was a simple man who turned his back on wealth and fame to help mankind.

He was born on the farm of Moses and Susan Carver, near Diamond, Missouri. Carver himself was never sure of his exact birth date or many details of his early life. His mother was a slave, purchased in 1855 for $700 at the age of thirteen, and he believed his father was a slave from a neighboring farm who was later killed in an accident while hauling a load of wood to town with an ox wagon.

The Civil War devastated southwest Missouri as warring factions struggled for power. Guerilla raids, lynching and bloody combat were commonplace occurrences. Shortly after his birth, Carver, his sister, and mother were kidnapped in a Confederate raid and taken to Arkansas for resale, as booty to fill the guerillas' war chest. Moses Carver sent a bounty hunter after the stolen slaves, but only George was recovered. Some reports say his mother was killed or died while a captive, while others claim she was taken away and sold.

Moses and Susan Carver took George and his brother Jim into their home and raised them as their own. In later years, Carver often recalled the love and guidance they gave him. As a young child, Carver's health was very frail, but his mind was always active. He spent hours roaming the nearby woods collecting plants and flowers, which he brought home to transplant. To the young boy, these plants were his friends, and he recalled weeping with sorrow if he broke a petal or stem. Carver had an uncanny ability with plants and they thrived under his care to the point that he became known locally as "the Plant Doctor."

Carver was born with a thirst for knowledge. Education was segregated and there were no colored schools nearby, so he walked eight miles to town every day to attend classes. By the age of 12 he had learned all he could locally and began a 20 year struggle for education, moving from Missouri to several towns in Kansas, where he worked and studied everything from basic skills to Latin and Greek. In Kansas City he attended a business college, mastering typing and shorthand. Carver was turned away from Highland College because of the color of his skin. He ended up attending Simpson College in Indianola, Iowa, where he supported himself by taking in laundry. Carver was the first black student to attend the school. He eventually earned a degree in agricultural science from Iowa Agricultural College (now Iowa State University), while working as the school janitor. Two years later he received his master's degree from the same school, and became the first African American to serve on its faculty. Carver always had the ability to make friends, and all of his life he recalled the many generous people who helped a poor black boy survive and get an education. Carver was also an accomplished artist, and his paintings were displayed at the 1893 Chicago World's Fair.

Carver began a promising career as a research botanist at Iowa Agricultural College, but the course of his life and the nation's agriculture changed when Booker T. Washington convinced him to come to the small Tuskegee Institute in Alabama, where Carver would find a home and spend most of his working life.

At that time, the South was still in ruins from the Civil War, and the farmlands were nearly useless, their soil depleted by generations of cotton farming. Carver realized new crops were needed to revitalize the agricultural industry. He wanted to help the small one-horse farmer who was struggling to survive on a few acres. He began a lifelong quest to develop new crops, the results of his research making a tremendous impact on the nation's economy. Carver found hundreds of uses for soybeans and peanuts, both as food products and in industry. He revolutionized the southern agricultural economy with over 325 products that could be made from peanuts, and by 1938 peanuts had become a $200 million industry and the main product of Alabama farms. Carver went on to find over 100 different products derived from the sweet potato. His lifelong research created a new economy, raising the South from ruin on the strength of her native resources.

As Carver's achievements became known, he was flooded with attention and offered lucrative research positions with some of the giants of industry, but he turned them all down, choosing instead to remain at Tuskegee, where he was paid only a tiny fraction of what he could have received, but where he felt he was doing the most good. Though he held three patents, Carver did not patent most of the discoveries he made at Tuskegee, saying "God gave them to me, how can I sell them to someone else?" He lived a simple life at Tuskegee, his home a single dormitory room, where he cooked on a hot plate. Yet his frugal lifestyle allowed him to save quite a bit of money. In 1938 he donated over $30,000 to the George Washington Carver Foundation, and willed the rest of his estate to the organization to carry on his work after his death. When he died on January 5, 1943 he was buried on the Tuskegee Institute campus he knew and loved so well.

The farm where Carver was born and raised near Diamond, Missouri is a now the George Washington Carver National Monument. Visitors can see displays from Carver's early life, walk the trails he explored as a youth, and learn more about the simple beginnings of a great man.

A trip to the monument starts with the Visitor Center, where a small museum holds information on Carver's work and his early life. Included are displays of some of the products he developed, a bed Carver slept in while attending school, and many historical artifacts from Missouri's Civil War days. There is also a film on Carver's life.

Outside the Visitor Center is a bust of Carver, where by pushing a button you can hear a recording of Dr. Carver reading the poem *Equipment*, in which he expresses his belief that we can all achieve the goals we set for ourselves. A meandering path loops through the farm for a distance of a mile or so, passing the site where Carver was born. Further down the path is a statue of Carver as a young boy, contemplating all the wonders that life held for him to discover.

The path leads to the house Moses Carver built in 1881. Though George Washington Carver never lived in this house, he visited Moses and Susan Carver here after he left the farm. From the farm house, the path leads through a grove of persimmon trees. Carver recalled in later years how as boys he and his brother would get into trouble for sneaking out of the house at night to eat persimmons. The Carver family cemetery holds the graves of Moses and Susan Carver, as well as other family members and slaves. The ages shown on the tombstones reflects the harsh times experienced in early days in this region. The path passes through a prairie that has been preserved much as it was in Carver's time and back to the Visitor Center. The walk is easy, with no steep slopes, and the path is well maintained, though not suitable for a wheelchair since it is dirt and gravel in some places.

A visit to the George Washington Carver National Monument is a great opportunity to get to know the origins of the man who rose from slavery to national prominence, and the work he accomplished to benefit all mankind, regardless of race.

The monument is located 2½ miles west of Diamond, Missouri, a few miles south of Interstate 44 near Joplin. The parking lot will accommodate smaller RVs, but it might be better to park a large rig elsewhere and drive a tow vehicle.

The Long Walk
The tragedy of the Navajo people

Whenever pioneers attempt to invade new territory, those people already present are going to resist to preserve their culture and protect their homeland. So it was with the Navajo and Apache Indians of New Mexico and Arizona.

The two tribes share a common Athabascan ancestry, though their cultures are very different. While the Apache were nomadic warriors, the Navajo followed the Pueblo example, learning to farm and herd sheep. They made their home in the rugged and vast land of canyons and mesas that stretched out from the Rio Grande River to the Grand Canyon.

As White settlers began to encroach onto their lands, conflict followed and the Navajo began to raid settlements, homesteads, and wagon trains. In 1851 the Army built Fort Defiance about 30 miles southeast of Canyon De Chelly in Arizona. Land where the Navajo had raised sheep was taken over to graze Army horses, further raising tension that escalated into a long series of Indian raids and reprisals by the soldiers. The violence peaked in 1860 when over a thousand Navajo warriors attacked Fort Defiance, resulting in its abandonment, followed by a campaign of revenge by the Army. Soldiers rampaged across Navajo lands, burning crops, killing livestock, and cutting down any Indian who tried to resist. With much of their livelihood destroyed, the Navajo were in danger of starvation.

A peace treaty was signed in 1861 that promised, among other things, government rations for the tribe and protected lands. The distribution of the rations was a festive event that included singing, dancing, and horse racing. When a soldier who cheated in one race was declared the winner, the mood changed and the soldiers retreated to the fort, where their commander ordered them to open fire. More than 30 Indians were killed, most women and children. Thus began a new wave of violence, each raid and attack bringing harsh reprisals from the military.

With the outbreak of the Civil War, many soldiers stationed on the western frontier were called to duty to fight in the east and south. General James H. Carleton, commanding the military in Arizona and New Mexico, realized the troop withdrawal would leave settlers unprotected and give the Indians an opportunity they could exploit to retake their lands. Carleton developed a plan to move the Indians to a reservation where the Army could control them. He chose a place on the high plains of eastern New Mexico called Bosque Redondo for his reservation.

For over a century, Bosque Redondo (round wood), located on the Pecos River, had served as a trading post where Spaniards and Mexicans traded with Apache and Comanche Indians, bartering blankets and supplies for silver, turquoise, and gold. Carleton persuaded President Abraham Lincoln to set aside 13,000 acres to build a reservation and fort to house the Navajo and Apache. He named the post Fort Sumner, after General Edwin Vose Sumner, under whom Carleton had served at one time.

Carleton chose Colonel Christopher (Kit) Carson to carry out his plan to conquer the Indians. Carson was known for his ruthless treatment of Indians and was just the man for the job. Ordered to kill any Apache man who resisted his troops, and to take all women and children prisoner, Carson quickly rounded up about 500 Mescalero Apache and transported them to Bosque Redondo. He then turned his attention to the Navajo.

Carson and his troops stormed into Canyon de Chelly and rousted the Navajo from their hogans, issuing the ultimatum, "Surrender or die." The soldiers cut down over 1,200 peach trees, burned the Navajo crops, slaughtered their livestock, and shot any Indian who tried to resist. Over two million pounds of corn the Indians had harvested was destroyed. Carson ordered the Navajos' homes, clothing, and all of their possessions burned. Indians who tried to hide in the caves of the canyon walls were hunted down and killed or captured.

Highway History And Back Road Mystery

Starved and beaten into submission, about 8,000 Navajo men, women, and children were then forced to make a grueling 400 mile trek to Bosque Redondo. Weak and starving, ill prepared for the harsh forced march, many Indians died on the trail. The soldiers beat and prodded them with bayonets as they stumbled along, and shot any Indian who could not go on.

Their troubles were not over once the Navajo arrived at Bosque Redondo. Their old enemies the Apache were already at the camp, and there were clashes between the two tribes. Food was in short supply, and promised rations did not arrive. Firewood was scarce, and the water was unfit to drink.

The men were soon put to work making adobe bricks to build the fort. Carleton had envisioned "civilizing" the Indians by teaching them Anglo farming methods, and they planted crops of corn, beans, melons, pumpkins, and wheat, along with some 12,000 cottonwood trees. Cutworms ravished the cornfields, while drought and hail seemed to conspire to work against the Indians. Most of the crops failed in the harsh soil of Bosque Redondo.

By the fall of 1864 there were about 9,000 Navajo at Fort Sumner, and conditions were terrible. Promised supplies of food, blankets, and clothing never arrived. The prisoners were living in whatever crudely improvised shelters they could create, without heat and almost no rations. The Indians, already weak and malnourished, became sick from the bad water and poor food. Every day brought new deaths from sickness and starvation. The soldiers assigned to guard them were a loutish lot unfit for military service anywhere else, and the treatment of their captives was often cruel. Over time some 3,000 Navajo would die at the concentration camp.

In 1865 the Mescalero Apache who were still able to walk fled the fort and returned to their homes further west. The soldiers did not care enough to pursue them.

Finally, in June, 1868, the government agreed to recognize the right of the Navajo people to their homeland and allowed them to leave Bosque Redondo. A peace treaty was signed granting the Navajo a 3.5 million acre reservation. During their imprisonment, the tribe had lost a fourth of the people to starvation and disease. At dawn on June 18, 1868, a column ten miles long left Fort Sumner, made up of 7,034 Navajo, 1,500 horses and mules, 2,000 sheep and a cavalry escort. The Navajo began their long walk home.

Today Fort Sumner is a State Historical Monument, with a small museum holding displays on the Navajo internment and a few re-created foundations to outline what remains of the camp. A walking tour leads visitors through the grounds, where signs tell the story of the Navajo confinement. The old fort is located about five miles from the present town of Fort Sumner, New Mexico and is open daily. There is a small admission charge.

A hundred years after they left Fort Sumner, a group of Navajo returned to reenact the signing of the peace treaty that finally freed their people, and erected a monument of stones from the Navajo reservation to help others remember the Long Walk.

White Dove Of The Desert

They call her the White Dove of the Desert, and for centuries she has been a beacon of Christianity to the people of southern Arizona. But the beautiful San Xavier del Bac Mission is much more than simply a church. Her story chronicles that of European exploration and settlement in the Southwest and reflects the history of the Native peoples who were here before, and the effect the newcomers had on their culture.

In 1692 Father Eusebio Francisco Kino, a Jesuit priest, traveled through the Sonora Desert on his way to California. Father Kino discovered a friendly Pima Indian village near present-day Tucson and stopped to introduce the villagers to the Church. The Pima Indians, also known as Tohono O'Odam, were receptive to his teachings and the priest founded a small church before continuing onward in his trek west. Father Kino liked the new converts at what he named San Xavier and returned many times as he explored and established missions in the region.

Over the next century different priests were either stationed at the mission or visited regularly. Religious services were held in a small, simple church at first and construction began on the building we know today in 1783.

Arizona was a harsh and dangerous land, and marauding Apaches raided many Pima villages, but for some reason never attacked San Xavier. Summers in the desert were nearly unbearable, and winters could bring frosts that damaged crops. But the small mission endured.

There was a lot of distrust between the Spanish crown and the Jesuits, and later when Mexico took control of the area in about 1828, the Mexican government demanded an oath of loyalty from the Spanish priests throughout the region. Many refused and were expelled, including the priest at San Xavier, and the mission was abandoned.

Over the next thirty years the church began to decay, though the Pima people tried to preserve what they could. During the Gold Rush of 1849, many travelers on their way to the gold fields of California stopped at San Xavier and wrote their names on the church's walls. A visitor in 1858 noted in his diary that the church's door was always left open and that birds had nested inside.

San Xavier saw new life with the Gadsden Purchase of 1859, when Arizona became part of the United States. By this time, the church's walls were crumbling and the roof leaked. The mission became part of the Santa Fe Diocese, and a restoration program began and a priest was assigned on a permanent basis. A school was established at the mission and continues to educate Pima children today. Saving the old mission would be a long term project.

Highway History And Back Road Mystery

Over the centuries, San Xavier has seen many changes. Construction of the mission and later restoration took place over a long period of time. For the first 120 years the White Dove of the Desert was not white at all, but a light tan color. Photographs of the mission from the late 1800s show streaked walls and many crude attempts at patchwork in the stucco. Tucson Bishop Peter Bourgade began an improvement project in 1889, making many repairs and additions to the mission complex.

In 1906 Tucson Bishop Henry Granjon took over the massive project of renovating the long-neglected church. Under Bishop Granjon's direction walls were restored, the mission and its outbuildings were painted and improved, and the original dirt floor was covered with pine flooring from Oregon. The bricks of the mission's unfinished east tower were plastered over and Granjon added an archway that frames the north entrance to the mission patio. The bishop was so involved in the project that it was not uncommon to see him in work clothes helping with the hard manual labor. Bishop Granjon was largely responsible for breathing new life into the crumbling mission and transforming it into the beautiful gleaming white structure that we know today.

One of Bishop Granjon's personal passions was for lions, perhaps a tribute to his original home in Lyon, France. Two lions had guarded the altar inside the church since 1797. Granjon included many plaster lions in his restoration work, looking down from the decorative scroll of the roof line, and two 400 pound metal lions guarded the entry to the Lourdes grotto Bishop Granjon built on top of a hill just east of the mission in 1908. Eventually most of the lion heads were removed as restorers worked to bring San Xavier back to her original design. Those that remain are blackened metal ones that adorn part of the arched rear entry. The entire community was outraged in 1982 when the two lions guarding the altar were stolen. Local art patron Gloria Giffords arranged for two replicas to be carved, with gold leaf on their manes and tales, and installed them where the original lions had stood guard for nearly 200 years.

Highway History And Back Road Mystery

There are many stories and legends about San Xavier Mission and its construction. The original church was built about a mile from the present location, but nobody knows why the site was changed when construction began in 1783.

Many stories concern the unfinished east tower. The original construction of the mission was undertaken with a 7,000 peso loan. Some say the tower was never finished because the project ran out of money. Others believe that after a workman fell to his death during construction of the tower, the superstitious workers refused to enter it again to complete the job. Legend has it that the worker who was killed turned into a giant rattlesnake and still lives under the unfinished tower.

Yet another claim is that Spain did not tax unfinished structures. There was discord between the Jesuits and Spain during this period, and the tower was never completed to avoid having to pay taxes. A University of Arizona historian rebukes that story by reporting that Spain gave religious orders ten years to establish a mission and teach the Indians Spanish. After that the mission became a full-fledged church and the Indians would be taxed. During the mission status, the Spanish treasury supported the mission, creating a drain that could not go on, and leaving the tower unfinished would not exempt San Xavier from taxation.

In a 1950 history of San Xavier, a Franciscan missionary named Celestine Chinn wrote about the mission's rigid symmetry of baroque design. Chinn noted that a doorway in the nave is balanced with a painting of a similar door on the opposite wall. The door to the sacristy behind the main altar is also balanced with a painted door exactly opposite. Chinn speculated that the original builders deliberately left the tower unfinished to offset the rigid symmetry found everywhere else in the mission.

In 1969 a workman removed a brick plug and discovered a doorway giving access to an unknown stairway leading up to the unfinished tower. Does the stairway hold any answers to the unfinished tower's secrets?

The tower was not the only thing left unfinished, lending support to the claim that funds simply ran out before the work was completed. In the baptistry, artists penciled in the outlines of frescos that were never finished. A sculpted drapery over a statue niche was never painted.

A certain amount of whimsy was included in San Xavier's design. One of the most popular stories is that of the cat and mouse incorporated into the church's facade. Perched on the curve of sculpted scrolls high above the main entrance are a mouse on the left and a cat on the right side, exchanging menacing glares as they have for centuries. The Tohono O'Odam say that when the cat finally manages to catch the mouse, the world will end.

Visitors are enchanted with the beautiful white exterior of San Xavier, but once they get inside they are often left speechless by the magnitude of its ornate decoration. Nobody knows exactly who is responsible for the elaborate artwork inside the church, though at least three different artists are represented. Almost every available space in the interior has a painting or sculpture of folk or religious origin, gold leaf, or plaster design. The sheer amount of artwork on the walls and ceiling is breathtaking, and even though the colors have faded some over the years, they are still spectacular.

Catholic church services are still held at San Xavier daily at 8:30 a.m., and Sundays at 8, 9:30, and 11 a.m. and at 12:30 p.m. Visitors are always welcome and many times fill the mission on Sunday mornings.

The mission complex also includes a museum displaying many artifacts of the church's early days. Visitors can see old gowns, books, and dishes used at San Xavier over the centuries, old photographs and maps of the area, and learn more about San Xavier's history. A small gift shop offers southwestern gifts and souvenirs.

Restoration and maintenance are an ongoing process at San Xavier. Decades of dirt and soot from devotional candles create a thick buildup on the church's walls and statues, and cleaning is done on a regular basis to combat the soot. The mission's exterior is whitewashed on a regular schedule to keep it gleaming under the desert sun or moonlight.

Highway History And Back Road Mystery

Visitors are always welcome to San Xavier. During the winter months you will find more people than the summer, when it can get very hot inside. Inside, visitors can listen to a tape giving an oral history of the mission.

San Xavier del Bac Mission is located seven miles south of Tucson, off of Interstate 19. A marked exit leads to the mission, which is easy to spot from the highway. There is adequate room to park an RV, and admission is free. After you tour the mission, be sure to treat yourself to some of the traditional Tohono O'Odam food sold at stands around the mission. My favorite is the Indian fry bread, a thick dough dropped into hot oil to create a delicious crispy bread, which is topped with beans, red chile, or sweets such as powdered sugar, cinnamon, or honey. A craft mall directly across from the mission is a good place to shop for Indian jewelry, baskets, and blankets.

Old Ironsides
America's Proudest Warship

Though the United States may have won her independence from Great Britain with the Revolutionary War, the fledgling nation was far from being a force to be reckoned with. In fact, if anything, sovereignty made America prey to any foreign power who chose to bully the tiny new country around. Without the might of the British crown to protect her, America was at the mercy of any and all who would take advantage.

Since much of America's early economy depended on foreign trade, our merchant ships were the key to growth and prosperity. Without the ability to conduct worldwide commerce, the rich natural resources of the United States could not be used to foster the growth the new country needed. It quickly became obvious that the country needed a navy to protect her interests abroad and to defend her shores.

On March 27, 1794 Congress passed a bill to establish the United States Navy, and authorized the construction of six frigates, one of which was the *USS Constitution*. Built at Hart's Shipyard in Boston, the new warship was designed to be powerful enough to defeat an enemy ship of the same class and fast enough to elude a larger adversary. Launched on October 21, 1797, the ship cost $302,718, a sum in dollars of the time that is comparable to the price of an aircraft carrier today. With an overall length of 204 feet, capable of carrying over 42,000 square feet of sail, and armed with over 50 cannon, *Constitution* was an impressive vessel. Her crew consisted of 450 sailors and Marines, as well as 30 young boys whose duties included hauling gunpowder and cannonballs to the gunners.

The frigate quickly went to work. In 1798 French ships were

conducting raids on American shipping along our coast and in the West Indies. Relations between the two countries had deteriorated to the point where all treaties had been broken and war seemed imminent. Under Captain Samuel Nicholson, *Constitution* put to sea to halt the attacks. Though her size made her unfit for the shallow waters of the West Indies that the French privateers preferred hunting in, *Constitution's* presence was enough of a threat to cause them to seek other targets, and American vessels were no longer molested.

For centuries a confederation of North African countries had controlled shipping in the Mediterranean Sea. Morocco, Tunis, Algiers, and Tripoli levied tribute on even the most powerful of European nations. Known as the Barbary Pirates, the ships of this confederation attacked any foreign vessel that did not pay the outrageous bribes they demanded, seizing the ships and their cargos and forcing the crews into slavery. The new United States was no exception, our ships frequently being captured or disappearing in the region, even though the young country had paid over $1 million dollars demanded by Algiers. In 1801, when the Bashaw of Tripoli realized that the Dey of Algiers had received more bribe money than he did, he declared war on the United States.

With *Constitution* as his flagship, Commodore Edward Preble brought a fleet of warships into the Mediterranean in 1803 and blockaded the port of Tripoli. The American force bombarded shore fortifications and enemy gunboats, receiving some fire in return. *Constitution's* mainmast was struck and she suffered some damage to her rigging and sails, but before long the Bashaw realized his gunboats were no match for the American fleet. On June 3, 1805 a peace treaty was signed in *Constitution's* cabin, the American captives held in Tripoli were released, and the payment of tributes were halted. The next stop was Tunis, where the American fleet dropped anchor and demanded a treaty that was quickly signed. *Constitution* had played an important role in making the Mediterranean safe for commercial shipping.

When the War of 1812 began, Great Britain had the most powerful navy in the world, with over a thousand vessels, compared to America's puny seventeen warships. The English were disdainful of the American Navy, believing our ships were too heavy and clumsy for rapid maneuvering in battle. It did not take them long to realize how wrong they were.

Soon after the war began, *Constitution* encountered a squadron of five British warships, including the 38-gun frigate *HMS Guerriere*. They gave chase, and though there was little wind to fill her sails, *Constitution* managed to slip away after an exchange of cannon fire.

About a month later, on August 19, 1812, *Constitution* again met HMS *Guerriere* near the Gulf of St. Lawrence, but this time the British warship was alone. The *Guerriere* began firing when the *Constitution* was still far astern, but the American commander, Captain Isaac Hull, held his fire and closed quickly with the foe.

Volley after volley roared from the *Guerriere*, but Hull waited until the ships were side by side before ordering "Now, boys, pour it into them!" A full broadside tore into the British ship, followed almost immediately by another. As *Constitution* raked her decks and rigging, the mizzen mast fell away and men on the *Guerriere* died in agony. Return fire from the *Guerriere* merely bounced off the heavy sides of the American ship. A British sailor cried out "Huzza! Her sides are made of iron!" From that moment on, *Constitution* would be known as *Old Ironsides*.

The battle was vicious, but over quickly. Within 35 minutes *Guerriere's* masts were shot away and she lay a crippled hulk. The British captain struck his flag and surrendered. The ship was so heavily damaged that after bringing the crew to the *Constitution*, the British frigate was burned. The enemy had suffered 78 sailors killed or wounded, while the *Constitution* lost fourteen men in what was one of the shortest naval battles in history.

The victory was an overwhelming boost for America's image in the eyes of the world. In little over half an hour the new nation that had been scorned had become a power to be respected. Back at home, the people were inspired with fresh confidence and felt a new sense of national pride. For *Constitution*, more glory lay ahead.

Highway History And Back Road Mystery

A few months later, on December 29, 1812, *Constitution,* under command of Commodore William Bainbridge, was off the coast of Brazil when she came across the British frigate *HMS Java.* The ships exchanged broadsides and *Constitution* had her wheel shot away, but her crew managed some clever maneuvering to stay in the battle. Within two hours the *Java's* captain had been killed along with 160 other of her crew who were killed or wounded. Her masts were gone and she lay helpless. Her crew surrendered and were brought aboard *Constitution*, then *Java* was set afire.

Following an overhaul in Boston, *Constitution* set to sea once again in December, 1814, slipping past a British blockade of Boston Harbor under cover of bad weather and poor visibility. Her last battle took place on February 15, 1815, when she spotted two British ships off the island of Madeira. The frigate *HMS Cyana* and sloop *HMS Levant* were no match for the American warship, and after a four hour battle they both surrendered.

With the war over, the battle scarred old veteran underwent extensive repairs before returning to sea to make two cruises to the Mediterranean. But time and hard service had taken their toll, and in 1830 *Constitution* was determined to be unseaworthy and condemned.

Plans to dismantle the old warship were set aside when Oliver Wendell Holmes published his poem *Old Ironsides*, rousing so much public sentiment that funds were made available to rebuild her. She became the first ship to enter the dry dock at the Boston Navy Yard.

Back on duty, *Constitution* made many peacetime voyages from 1835 to 1855, including a 495 day cruise around the world, in which she logged 52,279 miles. In 1849, while on a stop in Naples, Italy, Pope Pius IX visited the ship, making him the first Pontiff to step foot on United States territory.

By the Civil War, steamships like the ironclad *Monitor* were replacing the old wooden ships. For years *Constitution* served as a training ship, and she made her last trip abroad in 1878, carrying exhibits to the Universal Exposition in Paris.

By 1905 her timbers were rotting away, and the Navy made plans to destroy the old warship, but again a public outcry arose and she was saved. Starting in 1925, schoolchildren began sending in pennies and nickels to fund a major renovation, and the rest of the country soon pitched in to raise the money to bring her back to her former glory.

Since 1934, *Old Ironsides* has been berthed at the Charlestown Navy Yard near Boston, and today she is a living memorial to our seafaring history and a monument to the men who helped preserve our freedom. *Constitution* remains a commissioned ship of the United States Navy, making her the oldest commissioned warship in the world. She is crewed by active duty sailors, and every year makes a Turnaround Cruise on the Fourth of July, when she sails out of the harbor, fires her cannon in a National Salute to freedom, then returns to her berth.

Administered by a cooperative effort between the United States Navy and the National Park service, *Old Ironsides* is open to tours daily. Sailors lead visitors on an hour long tour of the ship and explain her history and the role she played in making this country a

Highway History And Back Road Mystery

major world power.

The tour is free, and the sailor who conducted our tour was both knowledgeable and an interesting guide. Starting at the bow, he explained the ship's rigging and pointed out the fighting top on each mast where Marine snipers were posted to fire down on the decks of enemy ships in battle. The ship's main mast is 220 feet long from keel to top. Our guide explained the construction techniques and materials that made *Constitution* so strong and formidable, and showed us the ship's bell, cast by Boston's own Paul Revere.

Leading us below to the gun deck, we learned how horrible conditions could be for men in battle at sea, and of their daily lives and duties when not engaging the enemy. The gun deck holds thirty 24-pound cannon, each weighing over three tons, capable of piercing twenty inches of wood at a thousand yards. At the rear of the gun deck is the Captain's Quarters, where Pope Pious IX and other dignitaries were entertained when visiting the ship.

The sailors assigned to duty as tour guides are dressed in uniforms of the era when *Constitution* put to sea to meet and defeat enemy warships. In all of her battles, no one ever managed to board *Old Ironsides*. Never in her proud history did one enemy step on her decks, except as a prisoner of war.

The ship has been maintained in original condition, though through her various renovations, only about ten percent of the original construction remains. The cannon and much of the other equipment is almost all original, carefully maintained by the sailors assigned to her.

The USS Constitution Museum at Charlestown Navy Yard has excellent exhibits on the ship's history, and a free video tells the story of the ship and the men who served on her. Many of the displays are interactive, giving visitors an opportunity to not only see, but to participate. There is no admission fee, though donations are welcome. The museum also includes a small gift shop and book store.

As anywhere in the metropolitan Boston area, parking near Charlestown Navy Yard is hard to find and expensive. Park in one of the outlying communities and take public transportation into Boston, and then to the Navy Yard for a tour of U.S. history you won't soon forget.

Highway History And Back Road Mystery

The Whitman Tragedy

Whenever one culture attempts to impose its ways on another, the opportunity for conflict and tragedy exists. When this happens, even the most innocent can suffer. Such were the events that led up to the 1847 outburst of violence in what is today eastern Washington at Waiilatpu, the site of the Whitman Mission. When it was over, thirteen people were dead. Ensuing events would lead to more deaths, both White and Indian.

The Reverend Marcus Whitman was called to the Oregon Territory in 1835 as a representative of the American Board of Foreign Missions, charged with the duty of bringing Christianity to the Cayuse Indians. Whitman, along with his new bride Narcissa, and the Reverend Henry Spalding and his wife, Eliza, along with William Gray, were westward bound in covered wagons.

Narcissa Whitman and Eliza Spalding became the first White women to cross the country overland. Reaching the Columbia River, the Whitmans traveled to Waiilatpu, near Walla Walla, and opened their mission. The Spaldings opened another mission at Lapwai, 110 miles east in Nez Perce country.

The missionaries learned the Indian language and attempted to convince the Cayuse to abandon their nomadic lifestyle and settle down as farmers, with little success. Slowly the mission grew, and a gristmill and several large adobe structures were built.

Frustrated with the lack of progress in getting the Indians to accept their brand of worship, in 1842 the American Board of Foreign Missions ordered the missions closed. But Whitman was a man of deep conviction, and he was not about to abandon his work. He made a remarkable overland journey during the winter, traveling through deep snow and crossing icy rivers to plead his case before the Board in Boston. Moved by Whitman's arguments, the Board rescinded its decision.

By this time the westward movement was in full swing, and more and more settlers were traveling along the Oregon Trail to new lands in the West. Whitman led the first wagon train all the way to the Columbia River on his return journey from Boston. The mission became an important stopping point for emigrants. Though the main route bypassed the mission by 1844, the sick and destitute knew they could find shelter with the Whitmans. Among those who found refuge were the seven Sager children, orphaned during the journey West. The Whitmans adopted the children.

Eleven years after Whitman established his mission, friction between the Indians and Whites was running high. The Cayuse saw more and more settlers crossing their land, and heard stories from other tribes about the Whites taking their lands. They saw the mission as a refuge for the newcomers. Strained relations took on even greater severity when a measles epidemic hit in 1847. While the emigrants responded to Whitman's medication and care, the Indians, with no resistance to the disease, died in great numbers. Within very little time, half the tribe had perished.

Convinced that Whitman was poisoning them to make way for the settlers, a band of Cayuse attacked the mission on November 29, 1847, killing Marcus and Narcissa Whitman and nine others, including the two Sager boys. About 50 survivors were taken captive. During their captivity, Louise Sager and two other children died of measles. The others were ransomed a month later. The massacre led to the closing of the Protestant missions in the Oregon country, and war between the Indians and settlers along the Willamette and Columbia Rivers. Before hostilities ceased, many more died on both sides.

Today the Whitman Mission is a National Historic Site, administered by the National Park Service, and is open daily except for Thanksgiving, Christmas, and New Years Day. Located just off Highway 12, about 15 miles east of Walla Walla, Washington, the monument includes a visitor center with a museum about the Whitmans and their Cayuse neighbors, as well as a small bookstore with several good books about the Oregon Trail and the Whitmans. A self-guided tour will take you through the mission grounds, past the old millpond and the Great Grave containing the victims of the massacre, and up to the top of the hill to the Whitman Memorial. The 27 foot monument, erected in 1897 on the 50th anniversary of the Whitmans' deaths, stands on the hill Narcissa used to climb to watch for her husband's return from his trips to minister to settlers and Indians. The path up the hill is steep, so be prepared. From the top is a very nice view of the surrounding countryside. There is a picnic area on the grounds, but no overnight camping is permitted.

Highway History And Back Road Mystery

Highway History And Back Road Mystery

The Ghosts Of Yuma Territorial Prison

Do convicts still haunt the old cellblocks?

Do you believe in ghosts? Do you think it is possible that the spirits of those long departed from this world can return? Are tales of ghosts and hauntings merely the product of overactive imaginations? Ask some of the rangers at Arizona's Yuma Territorial Prison State Historic Park, and you might learn that more than a few believe in ghosts. They have seen first-hand evidence!

The first seven inmates entered the Yuma Territorial Prison on July 1, 1876. Prison labor was used to build the cells they would live out their sentences in. Though the prison had a reputation as a "hell hole" it was actually very progressive for its time.

Prisoners had good medical care, a school was available, where many learned to read and write, and the prison had one of the first public libraries in Arizona Territory. In its latter days it had one of the first electric generating plants in the West, supplying power to the prison, and the excess electricity was sold to the city of Yuma. In their free time convicts made hand-crafted items, which were sold at public bazaars held at the prison on Sundays after church services. Prisoners were treated humanely, with punishments ranging from incarceration in a "dark cell" for infringement of prison rules, to having to wear a ball and chain for escape attempts. No executions ever took place at the prison, since in those days capital punishment was administered by county governments. Most prisoners did not serve out their entire sentences, since paroles and pardons were fairly easy to obtain.

Still, this *was* a prison, and many desperate men (and women) passed through its barred doors. A total of 3,069 prisoners, including 29 women, were incarcerated in the prison during its 33 years of operation. Their crimes included everything from murder and bank robbery to polygamy. Grand larceny was the most common conviction that brought inmates to Yuma. 111 prisoners died at the prison, most of those deaths caused by tuberculosis, a commonplace disease in Territorial days. Several others died from accidents, and eight were shot in escape attempts. Of the many prisoners who tried to escape over the years, only 26 were successful. While conditions were good for their times, they would be considered harsh by modern standards. Cellblocks were unheated, had no central cooling or plumbing, and prisoners slept on narrow wooden bunks with iron frames and straw filled mattresses alive with bedbugs.

One bold escape plan ended in a bloody battle when seven prisoners seized the prison's Warden Gates and several firearms, and tried to use him as a human shield to get past the guards. The hard bitten Gates would have none of this, and as they neared the sallyport leading outside of the prison, he ordered a tower guard to fire on the convicts and not to worry about hitting him. As rifle fire mowed down the prisoners, one viciously thrust a knife into the warden's back several times. Seeing the savage attack, a convict serving on trustee status grabbed a handgun from the warden's desk and shot the knife wielder dead. When the smoke had cleared, four of the fleeing convicts were dead and another wounded. Warden Gates survived the brutal attack, and the trustee who rescued him was paroled for his heroic actions.

A form of solitary confinement, the prison's " dark cell" was notorious. A narrow stone cell with a solid door and bare stone walls and floor, the only light and ventilation into the dark cell was a tiny opening high in the ceiling. There are stories that sometimes guards would get even with a particularly troublesome inmate by dropping a rattlesnake down through this opening to share his tiny space.

One of the prison's most celebrated guests was Pearl Heart, the girl bandit. An attractive young woman, Pearl was sent to the prison for holding up the Globe, Arizona stagecoach with a male partner. There are rumors that Pearl was released after she became pregnant in prison, a scandal no one wanted to acknowledge. She disappeared after she regained her freedom, and it is believed she later married a rancher in central Arizona and settled into a peaceful life.

By 1907 the prison was terribly overcrowded, and there was no room for expansion. Over the next two years the convicts were transferred to a new facility in Florence, Arizona, making the 200 mile trek on foot. The last prisoners left the prison in 1909. From 1910 to 1914 the prison housed the Yuma High School, and later the old cells provided lodging for hobos riding the rails through town. During the Great Depression, homeless families lived in the former prison. Over time the prison fell into disrepair and locals carried off many of the blocks from its walls for local building projects. Fires, weather, and the construction of the railroad further eroded the original prison site. Today the prison has been preserved as an Arizona State Historic Park, and the cells, main gate, and guard tower still stand to welcome visitors. But some claim that ghosts from the past are still there to greet tourists as well.

Over the years there have been many tales of ghostly sightings and eerie happenings at the old prison. One Yuma girl who attended high school classes at the old prison after the inmates were transferred to Florence claimed that a young man sat down beside her as she enjoyed her lunch outside one day, then disappeared when a classmate approached. A teacher reportedly refused to be on the grounds after dark after a mysterious experience he would not discuss.

Author Antonio Garcez, who wrote a story about Yuma Territorial Prison for the web site *Ghosts of the Prairie*, along with authoring a book on Arizona ghost stories, collected a number of stories of bizarre incidents at the prison from park rangers and visitors. Many of the stories revolve around the dark cell used for punishment.

One ranger at the park reported that she sensed a presence in a cell that frightened her, and also told of a photograph taken of a woman tourist during the 1930s that revealed the ghostly image of a man standing in the cell door behind her. That particular cell had been used to hold insane prisoners until they could be transferred to another facility.

While there is no record of any prisoner dying while in the dark cell, over the years two prisoners were taken from the cell directly to an insane asylum in Phoenix. There is also the story of a woman who was writing a magazine article on the prison and asked to be locked in the dark cell overnight to experience what prisoners endured there. Before long the writer was screaming to be released, claiming that there was someone else in the cell with her. Park rangers who came to her aid could find no one else in the tiny cell.

The prison also includes a very nice small museum, with displays of equipment used at the prison, photographs of convicts and guards, and other artifacts from Territorial days. The museum staff has reported that often things will be moved mysteriously from where they were left, lights turn on and off for no apparent reason, and reportedly on one occasion coins from the cash register in the museum gift shop flew into the air, then settled back in the drawer!

Is there any truth to these tales of otherworldly incidents? Do the spirits of men who served time at the old prison remain trapped within its walls? Or are these events that can be explained rationally? Why not visit Yuma Territorial Prison State Historic Park and draw your own conclusions?

Yuma Territorial Prison State Historic Park is located just off Interstate 8 in Yuma, Arizona, at the Fourth Avenue exit. The exit is clearly marked. The park is open every day but Christmas Day. Visitor Center hours are 8 a.m. to 5 p.m. Admission is $3 for adults. The Visitor Center, located in the museum, has drinking water and modern, handicapped-accessible restrooms.

Highway History And Back Road Mystery

Highway History And Back Road Mystery

Yulee Sugar Mill Ruins
A look into Florida's past

Just a couple of miles away from the busy commercialism of US Highway 19 in Homosassa, Florida, one can visit the remnants of a time long past. Nestled in a small wooded area are the ruins of the century old Yulee Sugar Mill, once a thriving plantation built by a man of peace who reluctantly found himself embroiled in the midst of America's bloodiest war.

The plantation's founder, David Levy Yulee, was one of Florida's most notable historic figures and helped shape the future of the state he adopted as his home. Yulee was born June 12, 1810 on the island of St. Thomas in the West Indies, the son of a prominent merchant. Seven years later the family moved to Florida and settled on 36,000 acres near Miscanopy. Yulee attended private schools in Virginia and studied law in St. Augustine.

An intelligent young man with a wide circle of friends and acquaintances, Yulee was appointed to Florida's first constitutional convention in 1838, and in 1841 he was elected as a territorial delegate to Congress. When Florida became a state in 1845, he was chosen as its first United States senator.

Yulee established a 5,100 acre plantation at Margarita, near the Homosassa River and married the daughter of the governor of Kentucky. His interests and activities ranged from politics and agriculture to building some of Florida's first railroads. Completed in 1860, his Atlantic and Gulf Railroad connected Fernandina on the Atlantic coast to Cedar Key on the Gulf coast.

Yulee seemed to prosper at whatever he did. By 1851 his sugar mill had a thousand workers and he imported state of the art machinery from as far away as New York to refine the sugar. The decade between 1851 and 1861 were perhaps the best years of Yulee's life.

Highway History And Back Road Mystery

He enjoyed business successes and a peaceful lifestyle at his plantation, overseeing the busy day to day operations, as well as developing new business enterprises.

The dawning of the Civil War forced Yulee to make a difficult choice between supporting the secession or siding with the Union. Though Yulee would have preferred to avoid war, and hoped for a peaceful solution to the debate, he agreed to serve in the newly created Confederate Congress. Even so, he resisted using his railroads to make connections that would better aid the war effort. However, Yulee found himself being pulled deeper and deeper into the conflict. His mill supplied sugar products to Southern troops and his mansion became a warehouse for ammunition and supplies.

Yulee's hopes of peace were ended in May, 1864, when a Union raiding party guided by one of Yulee's slaves burned his mansion on Tiger Island to the ground. The sugar mill, located inland, was not damaged, but never resumed operation after the war ended. Eventually it fell into ruins. Yulee himself was imprisoned in Georgia for two years, charged with aiding the escape of Confederate President Jefferson Davis.

After a presidential order from Ulysses S. Grant, Yulee was finally a free man, and he began to pick up the pieces of his pre-war life. He managed to resume his railroad interests, but never achieved the prosperity he had enjoyed before the war. He died in New York in 1886.

For years the old sugar mill sat abandoned, and in 1923 the mill and several surrounding acres were presented to the Citrus County Federation of Women, who in turn deeded it to the state in 1953. Hewn from native limestone, the mill has been partially restored and is under the administration of the Florida Department of Environmental Protection and is listed as an Historic State Park.

Today a large chimney still stands, and a forty foot long block extension houses the boiler. Several parts and pieces of the old machinery lay beside the mill. Yulee Sugar Mill is the only antebellum sugar mill in the United States. Visitors can tour the ruins at leisure, following a concrete path with interpretive signs. There is a nice sized parking area across the street from the old ruins. For more information on Yulee Sugar Mill Ruins State Historic Park, write c/o Crystal River Archaeological State Park, 3400 N. Museum Point, Crystal River, Florida 34428, or call 352-795-3817.

Highway History And Back Road Mystery

The Witches Of Salem

Start with a community of religious fanatics. Add in a large amount of ignorance, equal doses of lies and suspicion, a dash or two of human frailty, and a bit of jealousy and revenge. Blend above with ego and greed, mix in a climate of fear and intolerance, and you have the perfect recipe for what happened in Salem, Massachusetts in 1692. The result is an American tragedy of unimaginable proportions.

It all began in January, 1692 when a group of young girls in Salem, a village of approximately 550 residents, began exhibiting bizarre behavior, including seizures, cursing, screaming fits, and trance-like states. Their distressed Puritan community called in physicians to examine the girls, and when no physical cause could be determined for their outrageous behavior, it was decided by the community at large that it must be the work of the devil.

The community began praying and fasting to rid themselves of Satan's influence. The girls were questioned about who was controlling their minds, and eventually reported that three women were to blame. Two of the women named by the girls, Sarah Good and Sarah Osborne, denied any involvement, but were still imprisoned. The third of the accused was a slave named Tituba, who had been telling the girls stories of her homeland and tales of voodoo and witchcraft. Tituba claimed that there was a conspiracy of witches throughout the village.

In March the girls accused a fourth woman of practicing witchcraft. While Tituba and the other two women identified earlier were fringe members of the community, the latest suspect was Martha Corey, an upstanding member of the Puritan congregation. The community went into a panic. Obviously Satan's influence had penetrated deep into the very heart of Salem. Several more young women came forward and claimed that they too had been "possessed" by the witches among them.

The hysteria that followed continued for months, as neighbor accused neighbor and friend turned on friend. There is no doubt that old animosities and jealousies were brought into play as more and more people were brought before the Court of Inquiry. Many of the accused were women whose behavior had previously disturbed the community, or those of poor economic circumstances, but this was not always the case. Others were upstanding members of the church who had offended someone who now saw a way to exact revenge.

Some of those accused confessed, perhaps out of fear or under duress. Margaret Jacobs, who was arrested along with her grandfather George, testified that she was a witch, as were her grandfather and another man named George Borroughs. Later Martha claimed that she was told that if she did not confess, she would be hanged, but that if the admitted her crime her life would be spared.

The Court of Inquiry was far from a scientific body. Evidence included not only the testimony of the afflicted girls, but also supernatural attributes such as "witchmarks" and the reactions of the afflicted girls. During the examinations of the accused, the girls would sit in the courtroom and moan and thrash about, claiming that their behavior was being controlled by the witch on the witness stand. On some occasions the girls would mimic every movement of the accused. If a person on trial brushed a hand across their face, bowed their head, bit their lip, or shuffled their feet, the girls would copy the movement in unison. They also claimed that they could see specters hovering in the courtroom above the accused. The examiners accepted all of this as valid evidence and began passing guilty judgements and issuing death sentences.

Sarah Osborne died while in prison, on May 10, 1692. The first official execution took place on June 10, when Bridget Bishop was hanged, claiming her innocence even as the noose was slipped over her head.

Following the first execution the accusations rose to a fever pitch. The trials were not universally supported in Salem. Cooler heads among the community opposed the examinations and signed petitions in support of accused people they believed were innocent. Meanwhile, the witch hysteria had spread throughout Essex County, and witch trials began in all 34 towns and villages in the region. Hundreds were jailed. Some died in prison, while others went insane with fear.

One Salem clergyman, accused by the girls of being the Devil, fled to Maine, where he was captured and executed. Later another minister from Salem traveled to Maine, removed the dead man's head and brought it back for display in Salem.

On June 19 Rebecca Nurse, Susannah Martin, Sarah Good, Elizabeth Howe, and Sarah Wildes were executed. A month later George Jacobs, Martha Carrier, George Burroughs, John Willard, and John Proctor were hanged.

One month later, on September 19, Giles Corey was pressed to death for refusing to enter a guilty plea in his examination. His wife, Martha, was hanged days later, along with Mary Parker, Samuel Wardwell, Margaret Scott, Wilmott Redd, Ann Pudeator, Mary Easty, and Alice Parker.

Finally, on October 29, 1692 Massachusetts Governor Sir William Phips responded to the public outcry raised against the witch trials and dissolved the Court of Inquiry. No further executions took place, and eventually the people still imprisoned were released to try and pick up the pieces of their lives.

What was behind the Salem witch hysteria? Today some researchers claim that a mold in grain the girls had eaten had caused them to experience convulsions and hallucinations. While this may have been a contributing factor, there is no doubt that once the ball was rolling, some people used the growing panic to further their own agendas. Disagreeable neighbors, uncooperative business rivals, and ill-tempered relatives found themselves facing the cruel examinations of the Court of Inquiry.

Today Salem has turned into a gaudy tourist trap with one "witch museum" after another. Step up to the counter, pay your money, and you can walk through tacky wax museums, listen to costumed actors tell colorful tales of the days of the witch trials, or learn about spells and incantations from "real" witches. From the Salem Witch Museum to the Witch Dungeon Museum to the Salem Wax Museum to Salem Witch Village to the Witch History Museum to Dracula's Castle to Salem's Museum of Myths and Monsters to Boris Karloff's Witch Mansion and on and on ad nauseam you can be titillated, ripped off, and bored silly, depending on your level of intelligence and bank balance. As if that weren't enough, there are a half dozen or so ghost tours that are guaranteed to separate you from whatever stray coins that may still be left lurking in the deepest recesses of your pocketbook. Get the picture?

This is not to say that a trip to Salem is a total waste of your time. Quite the contrary. Salem has a rich history completely separate from the unfortunate witch messiness. From the earliest days of her settlement Salem looked toward the sea as a source of revenue.

By 1643 ships from Salem were ranging far and wide in search of trade. Single-decked sloops and schooners traveled as far as the West Indies, carrying cod and lumber to trade for rum and molasses, which was then traded in Europe for manufactured goods needed in the New World. Salem merchants and shipowners grew wealthy from their trading voyages until the Revolutionary War, when English tariffs cut deeply into their profit margins.

With no established navy to combat the British fleets, the Continental Congress authorized privateers to sail in search of enemy shipping. Salem put more ships and men to sea than any other port, and the privateers from Salem were able to take a heavy toll on British ships, further lining the pockets of their owners.

When the war ended, Salem's merchant fleet again set to sea carrying merchandise to distant ports as far away as China and India. Salem enjoyed its most prosperous period during this rich era. Trade from Salem helped to open up economic opportunities for the whole of the new nation.

Today the Salem Maritime National Historic Site, administered by the National Park Service, tells the story of Salem's rich maritime heritage, and the homes of some of the wealthiest ship owners and merchants have been preserved. The National Historic Site operates a museum in downtown Salem and has a smaller facility on the waterfront. Also along the waterfront is the Customs House, where a young Nathaniel Hawthorne once worked as a Customs Inspector, and the Hawkes and Derby houses, the homes of two of Salem's wealthiest merchant kings. A re-created merchant sailing ship is also on display nearby.

A few blocks away is the House of Seven Gables, made famous by Hawthorne in his novel by the same name. Built in 1668, the mansion is one of the few remaining Post Medieval houses in America. For an $8.50 admission fee, visitors can tour the mansion and its grounds and get an idea of how the upper crust lived in days gone by.

In total contrast to the many hokey tourist traps that call themselves museums, the Peabody Essex Museum is an excellent facility showcasing the history of Salem, her great maritime past, and fine artworks from around the world. The museum's collections include over 50,000 maritime objects, a wonderful selection of American decorative art, and one of the nation's finest collections of Asian art, along with fine displays of African art and the work of other cultures worldwide.

Salem is also home to the nation's oldest living history museum, Salem 1630: Pioneer Village, where costumed guides treat visitors to a re-created 17th century New England fishing village. As visitors walk through thatched roof cottages, watch the blacksmith work at his forge, or villagers work their gardens they will feel like they have truly stepped back in time. Admission to Pioneer Village is $7.50 for adults.

If you like historic old graveyards, be sure to stop at the Old Burying Point Cemetery, where many of the earliest settlers were laid to rest, including a judge from the witch trials and one who came across on the *Mayflower*.

In earlier times, the physical boundaries of Salem extended beyond the present day city limits. In nearby Danvers, away from the garish commercialism of Salem, are the homes of many of the participants in the witch hysteria, and a handsome monument erected in memory of the victims of the witch trials. Danvers is a quiet community which we found much more pleasant than Salem.

If you can look past the plastic and the fake to explore Salem's true heritage, you will find it to be an interesting place to visit. But it takes an effort to wade past all of the tourist traps and street corner psychics to find the true soul of the city.

Highway History And Back Road Mystery

Georgia's Paul Revere

We've all heard the tale of Paul Revere, the brave Boston silversmith whose midnight ride alerted patriots that the "British are coming!" The lesser known part of that story is that Paul Revere was actually captured before he completed his mission and two other riders went on to warn the Minutemen of the Redcoats' advance. But did you know that Georgia had its very own version of Paul Revere?

It happened on May 2, 1863 during the Civil War, when Union troops under Colonel Abel D. Streight began moving toward the town of Rome, Georgia with the intent of seizing the Confederate arsenal there, then cutting off the South's supply line between Atlanta and Chattanooga. Mail carrier John Henry Wisdom was at Gadsden, Alabama when he saw Streight's men moving forward for the impending raid and set off to rally resistance.

Setting off by horse and buggy in mid-afternoon, Wisdom made it to Gnatville, Alabama, a distance of about 22 miles, before his horse gave out. The only mount to be had was a lame pony owned by a local widow woman. Borrowing the pony, the brave rider continued on his mission. But the poor animal could only make it another five miles before Wisdom had to abandon it and ride off on another horse he managed to borrow.

Through the evening and on into nightfall Wisdom continued, riding one horse until it collapsed and then begging another wherever he could. On occasion farmers refused to loan him their animals and he continued on foot until he could find another farmhouse to stop and ask for help. At one point he stumbled on for miles before finding a mule he could use. Sometime late at night an exhausted John Wisdom arrived at the tiny settlement of Vanns Valley, Georgia, where he was able to get two fresh horses and race the final seventeen miles into Rome, completing a journey of nearly seventy miles on foot and horseback in just over eight hours.

It was after midnight when Wisdom arrived in Rome, but his night's work was still not done. Rousing the citizenry, he helped organize a hasty defense. Since Rome was 60 miles south of the Confederate lines, there were no troops on hand to protect the town. Assembling a motley collection of wounded soldiers, old men, and young boys, a battle strategy was formed.

Knowing the Union troops would have to come across a covered wooden bridge over the Coosa River to enter town, the defenders chose the span to make their stand. Filling the bridge waist deep with straw soaked in oil and barricading it with cotton bales, the plan was to hold out as long as possible in the hope that reinforcements would arrive, and as a last resort, to set fire to the bridge to hold the invaders at bay.

Meanwhile the call went out for help and planters and farmers began pouring into Rome from the surrounding countryside armed with squirrel guns and muskets, much as the Minutemen had at Lexington and Concorde nearly a century before. But unlike events in New England long before, this time bloodshed was averted.

At about 9 a.m. an advance force of 200 men led by a Captain Russell arrived at a hill overlooking the town and saw the defenses awaiting them. Unwilling to risk his men against such stubborn resistance, Russell withdrew and reported back to Colonel Streight that Rome was not to be taken easily. Streight began to move his force westward and they soon ran into Confederate General Nathanial Bedford Forrest and were captured. John Henry Wisdom's midnight ride had succeeded in saving Rome!

As a reward for his gallant actions, the citizens of Rome presented John Wisdom with an award of $400 and a beautiful silver service. Though there is no evidence that the silver service was created by that other midnight rider from Boston, it did not matter to John Henry Wisdom, local hero. His long ride was done and Rome was safe. That was reward enough.

Haunted New Orleans

Is there life after death? Do those who have gone on to the afterworld have the power to exert influences on our physical world? Some may scoff at the idea, but people in New Orleans might tell you different.

What is it about New Orleans that makes it the focal point of so many ghost stories and tales of the occult? Few American cities have the colorful history that New Orleans does. Pirates, slave traders, smugglers, soldiers, outlaws, gamblers, and adventurers have gravitated to the Crescent City from the first days Europeans discovered the Gulf Coast. Native peoples from North America, Africa, the Caribbean, and West Indies have added their influence to help shape the history and culture of one of the oldest cities in the country. At one time, New Orleans was a regular stopover for some of the most violent brigands in the Western Hemisphere. Many believe the spirits of more than a few of these colorful characters still inhabit the old buildings and wander the narrow streets and alleyways of the French Quarter.

Perhaps one reason for the city's reputation for things eerie is its famous cemeteries. Most of us may think of well trimmed grass and row after row of neat gravestones when we picture a cemetery. Not so in New Orleans' above-ground cemeteries. Enter St. Louis Cemetery No. 1 and you enter a labyrinth of tombs of all sizes, shapes, and conditions. Huge pristine marble tombs stand side by side with dilapidated knee high brick crypts. The grave of an adventurer from the early 1800s may sit beside that of a fallen Vietnam war soldier. Narrow pathways wind through the cemetery, passing well maintained tombs that are works of art, as well as others that aren't much more than crumbling piles of brick. It is a beautiful, serene, and haunting place.

These "cities of the dead" came into being two centuries ago, when New Orleans' high water table made traditional burial impractical. After the frequent floods the city experienced in its earlier days, it was a common occurrence to have caskets float back to the surface, both an upsetting and unhygienic experience. Modem drainage technology has alleviated the problem, but the tradition remains.

Aesthetics and culture also played a part in the popularity of the above ground cemeteries' tombs and mausoleums. Early settlers from Spain and France brought their own distinct architectural styles to New Orleans. These influences are reflected in many of the burial structures. Over time many of the tombs have fallen into disrepair, but these days the city is working hard to restore and upgrade the old cemeteries. This is due partly to the ever growing popularity and interest in the cemeteries with tourists. Many organized tours visit the cemeteries every day, where tour guides well versed in the city's history and culture relate tales of the wild old days and the people buried in the cemeteries.

Perhaps the most famous tomb in St. Louis Cemetery No. I is that of the voodoo priestess Marie Laveau, who died in New Orleans in 1881. Most visitors come to her grave to experience the thrill of being a part of unique history, while others come to the grave to perform a voodoo ritual of good luck, scratching an x on the face of her crypt. Others leave offerings of food to the departed voodoo leader. It is interesting to note that some doubt that Marie Laveau is even buried in the tomb - in the early days, the remains were often removed from tombs so the burial spaces could be reused. But to believers, it will always be Marie Laveau's tomb, and it will surely continue to draw thousands every year interested in voodoo and the occult.

It seems that every old building in the French Quarter has its own ghost story or resident ghost. The ghost stories, as all good ones do, always seem to revolve around some deep tragedy. A perfect example is that of the Octoroon Mistress.

The tale is one of unrequited love, in which a beautiful Creole woman named Julie was the mistress of a wealthy French gentleman. Julie was a rare beauty, a cultured woman who spoke both French and Spanish. In modern society, she would be considered a true prize. But in her day, Julie had a terrible cross to bear. She was an octoroon, meaning one of her great-grandparents were black. In those days, the mid-1800s, white gentlemen did not marry women from Creole society, no matter how desirable they were. But marriage was what Julie longed for.

Over and over she begged her lover to marry her, to no avail. Finally, when Julie threatened to end their affair, he relented, but with one condition. He asked Julie to prove her love for him by spending the night on the roof of her building naked. He rationalized his bizarre demand by telling Julie that she would be experiencing the abuse of the elements, just as he would have to suffer the social disgrace he would endure if they married. He didn't expect his beloved to accept his offer, but Julie went out onto the roof to begin her long night's ordeal.

The gentleman, if he can be called that, spent the evening drinking with friends, sure that his beloved had given up as soon as the temperature dropped. Eventually he went to Julie's bedroom, expecting to find her safe and warm under the bedcovers. But she was not in her bed. Stumbling up to the roof, his drunken state was quickly wiped away by the horrible sight of Julie's lifeless body lying frozen in the rain. Since that day, people have reported seeing the specter of a naked woman walking on the roof of Julie's building on cold and rainy December nights.

New Orleans' most notorious haunted building is located at 1140 Royal Street, the former home of Madame Delphine Lalaurie, a wealthy and prominent Creole woman, but one with a terrible hidden secret of cruelty.

On April 10, 1834, a fire broke out in Madame Lalaurie's elegant mansion. Madame Lalaurie directed firemen to remove expensive paintings and valuables, denying that anyone else was inside the home. When Madame Lalaurie refused to open locked doors for the firemen, they became suspicious and broke them down, making a horrible discovery. Several slaves were found inside the rooms in chains, suffering from terrible abuse. Among them lay the bodies of others who had already died. A local newspaper reported that the slaves had been confined in their dungeons for months, surviving on bread and water. They were constantly exposed to torture at the hands of their evil mistress, and "longingly awaited death as a relief from their suffering."

This was not the first time Madame Lalaurie had been accused of cruelty. Years earlier she had been fined for mistreating a young slave girl. The girl died under mysterious circumstances when she fell from the mansions's roof. Madame Lalaurie claimed the girl had fallen by accident, but witnesses testified that Madame Lalaurie was chasing her with a whip when the girl plunged to her death. As word spread of the ghastly discovery, an angry mob formed outside the mansion, calling for revenge. Suddenly the courtyard doors flew open and Madame Lalaurie charged out in her carriage and fled, never to be seen again.

Located at 1140 Royal Street, the former, home of Madame Lalaurie has been called the most haunted building in New Orleans. The home was abandoned for years, but was later used as a Union headquarters during the Civil War. Later it was a gambling hall and school. These days the mansion has been divided into several apartments. The building has a long history of hauntings, and the story of the fire and the horrible discovery of the slaves lives on. Many claim that some of the former occupants remain, including the young slave girl who fell from the roof. Over the years, there have been repeated reports of sightings of a girl teetering on the roof's edge or running in terror across the top of the building. Others have claimed to hear the keening of slaves long dead, and the rattling of their chains.

Are these macabre stories real, or the product of overactive imaginations? Who can say? Maybe the best way is to decide for yourself. The next time you're in New Orleans, take one of the city's many haunted history tours, or spend a few hours wandering through the old above ground cemeteries and visiting her old buildings. Listen carefully. Is that normal street traffic you hear, or is it some other, more mysterious sound? Perhaps the telltale words of some long ago adventurer whispering in your ear?

Highway History And Back Road Mystery

Poker Alice

The Old West was populated by a remarkably colorful collection of adventurers, dreamers, rebels, and misfits. It took men and women of outlandish character to be willing to explore new lands, endure the hardships that accompanied pioneer life, and survive under conditions far removed from what they were accustomed to back East. Maybe their methods and lifestyles were not quite what "polite society" was used to, but the characters who made their mark during our westward expansion painted the landscape and history in broad and brilliant patterns.

One such unforget-table character was Poker Alice of Deadwood, South Dakota, a hard drinking gambler, madam, and bootlegger whose antics earned her legendary status that lives on today.

A woman of unusual beauty in her youth, she was born Alice Ivers in Devonshire, England on February 17, 1853 and educated in the finest schools. When Alice was a young woman her family immigrated to the United States and settled in Colorado, where she married a mining engineer named Frank Duffield.

Duffield loved playing poker and taught his young bride the game. Alice proved herself to be a good student, and she seemed to have a natural skill for playing cards. In fact, the student soon outshined the teacher and Duffield found it hard to win against his bride.

By all accounts the marriage of Alice Ivers to Frank Duffield was a happy union, and many who knew her said that he was the great love of her life. But sadly, it was not to be a long relationship. Soon after they were married, Frank Duffield was killed in a mine accident in Leadville, Colorado.

Looking for a way to support herself and to ease her grief, Alice became a professional gambler and soon became a familiar face in the gambling halls of Colorado.

Alice met her second husband, Warren Tubbs, while in a card game, and he was smitten by the time the first hand was dealt. Anyone familiar with the term "unlucky at gambling, but lucky in love" has a good idea of Warren Tubbs' life. Though he considered himself quite the card shark, in actuality he usually lost much more than he ever won. Tubbs eked out a marginal living by painting houses and buildings, but it was Alice who was the real family breadwinner.

Call it luck or call it a natural talent for the pasteboards, but whatever it was, Alice had plenty of it. She was a consistent winner at high stakes poker, often raking in jackpots of as much as $6,000 in a single game!

Alice loved spending money just as much as she loved winning it, and her wild spending sprees in places like New York City were as legendary as her beauty. Many gamblers lured to her table by her good looks soon found themselves bankrupted by her good luck. But though she may have broken their bank accounts, Alice seems to have won their hearts, and she had a long list of admirers. Somewhere along the line she earned the nickname Poker Alice, which she would be known as for the rest of her life.

Though their relationship had plenty of problems, Alice always took care of Tubbs and defended him against any attack, verbal or otherwise, that his gambling might get him into. She carried a .38 revolver with her at all times and was not hesitant to use it. Yet she was willing to sit across from him at a poker table and empty his pockets time and time again.

During their long and often stormy marriage, the couple had

several children and drifted through the gambling halls of Deadwood, Rapid City, and Sturgis, South Dakota, supported by Alice's skill at the card tables. Stubbs was stricken with tuberculosis and Alice nursed him during his long illness until he died in South Dakota in 1910.

After a third brief marriage, Alice turned all of her energies to gambling, even operating her own gambling hall. For a time she did well, but over the years her luck seemed to decline and she turned to other means to support herself, including bootlegging and operating a brothel in Sturgis.

The latter years of her life were not kind to Poker Alice. Her youthful beauty vanished, the combined result of alcohol and the cigars she loved. The fine clothes she once bought in New York were replaced by weathered skirts and men's shirts. Alice's beauty, which had won so many hearts did not just fade, it disappeared, leaving behind a rough looking, tough talking hag. But she remained a favorite in the hearts of many and her legend has lived on long after her death on February 27, 1930.

Highway History And Back Road Mystery

The Mad Bomber of Bath

In a small park in the tiny community of Bath, Michigan there is a historical marker to a tragedy that would seem to be more in keeping with today's school massacres and terrorist attacks than the happier times of the "Roaring Twenties."

Located northwest of Lansing, Bath has never been a big town, but rather one of those small communities where everybody knows everybody and neighbors help each other during hard times. Perhaps that makes the events of May 18, 1927 even harder to understand.

55 year old Andrew Kehoe was a farmer and served as treasurer of the local school board. On the surface, Kehoe seemed to be a pillar of the community, but there were underlying problems and tensions that were about to lead to unspeakable horror.

Two years earlier, Kehoe had vigorously opposed a tax increase to raise funds for a new school. His arguments fell on deaf ears and the Bath Community Consolidated School was built. Since then, Kehoe had been struggling financially, behind on the mortgage on his farm and supporting a sick wife whose medical bills were mounting up higher every day.

He blamed his financial woes on the higher taxes imposed by the school levy. To stave off foreclosure Kehoe had been embezzling money from the school treasury, and he knew that things could not continue on forever. So he conceived a mad scheme to end all of his troubles and get back at those he felt had wronged him at the same time.

In the early morning hours of that unforgettable day, Kehoe set his plan in motion. First he used poison to kill all of the fruit trees on his farm, then he bludgeoned his wife to death. Next he detonated dynamite charges in his farmhouse, barn, and outbuildings. Little remained standing on the farm but for a fence upon which Kehoe had painted the words "Criminals are made, not born."

Driving into town, Kehoe paused long enough to sever the telephone lines, cutting Bath off from the rest of the world. Then he entered the new school building and placed a charge, later estimated to be at least 500 pounds, of dynamite in the basement. The deranged man then returned to his car and set off the bomb at 9:40 a.m.

The blast that followed was horrendous, ripping through the north wing that housed the school's third through sixth grades. The school's floors collapsed, windows shattered into deadly flying shrapnel, walls exploded, and the roof blew off. The building collapsed inward, trapping students and teachers inside, while many other victims were blown out into the schoolyard. The explosion killed 7 teachers and 38 students, and injured over 50 more.

As always seems to happen, heroes were created in the horror. School principal Floyd Huggett stumbled through the wrecked halls, choking blindly in the smoke and dust as he called out to students who had survived, leading them out of the building to safety. Teachers gathered injured and frightened students and carried them outside, while older children helped younger students find their way out of the wreckage.

Witnesses said Kehoe sat outside the school in his car gloating as torn bodies rained down around him. When school superintendent Emery E. Huyck ran up to Kehoe's car to confront him, the farmer fired a rifle into yet another bomb inside the vehicle, killing both himself and Huyck. Bath postmaster Glenn Smith and his father-in-law, Nelson McFarren, rushing to the scene, were also killed in the car bomb.

Rescue workers labored in the rubble for days searching for survivors, while investigators tried to piece together what had happened. They found that the damage could have been much worse. Kehoe had placed charges under virtually every classroom, but some of the wires had short-circuited and the charges failed to go off. If this had not happened, the death toll would have surely been much higher.

Highway History And Back Road Mystery

Investigators sifted through the debris of the school and Kehoe farm for weeks, finding evidence of the workings of the killer's deranged mind. The only motive they could determine was that Kehoe was apparently mad at the world and blamed the school board for all of his problems.

Few people remain today who remember the terrible events that took place that tragic morning in Bath, Michigan. A memorial park was erected at the site of the Bath Community Consolidated School, and today children play where others once suffered and died at the hands of the Mad Bomber of Bath.

Highway History And Back Road Mystery

Highway History And Back Road Mystery

The Pig War

The United States and Canada have enjoyed a long and friendly relationship. Our boundary with our neighbors to the north is the longest unguarded border in the world. But there was a time when a lowly pig almost brought the two nations to battle and had troops from both sides facing off with each other for more than a decade.

As is usually the case in such events, the pig actually played a very small role in a much larger controversy, but it was the excuse both sides needed to give them a reason to act.

It all began in 1859 on San Juan Island, now part of Washington state. A treaty in 1846 had established the border between Canada and the United States and decreed that the dividing line between the two countries would be the channel around San Juan Island. But there was one little problem – there were actually *two* channels, one on each side of the island! If the line was extended down Rosario Strait, San Juan Island would be Canadian Territory and fall under British control, but if the line followed Haro Strait, the island would be American. Citizens from both countries had settled on the island, and the Canadian Hudson Bay Company had a presence as well.

American authorities, demanding the British pay taxes, had come to San Juan Island at one point and attempted to seize a flock of sheep owned by the Hudson Bay Company to be sold at auction to satisfy unpaid taxes. What followed was a comedy of errors. No one stopped to consider that the sheep, being loyal British subjects, might object to this move. Or maybe the sheep just were not too enthused about riding in a rowboat and some Indian canoes the tax men had commandeered. Whichever the reason, the sheep butted the officials, ran off in every direction, and left the deputies red faced and frustrated.

Englishman Charles Griffin was employed by the Hudson Bay

Highway History And Back Road Mystery

Company and stationed on San Juan Island. A hot tempered red headed Irishman, Griffin raised pigs and felt his animals should be allowed to forage freely wherever they chose to. His neighbor, American Lyman Carter, took objection to the hogs rooting in his potato patch, and complained several times about the animals getting into his garden. Griffin brushed off his neighbor's complaints in a less than friendly manner.

Things came to a head on June 15, 1859 when Lyman Carter looked out his window and spotted one of Griffin's pigs in his garden again. He stepped outside and shot the animal dead. With tempers short on both sides at the time, British authorities threatened to arrest Carter and take him to Vancouver Island for trial. The Americans responded by calling on the army for help, and soon a detachment of soldiers commanded by Captain George Pickett arrived.

Not to be outdone, James Douglas, the British governor of Vancouver Island dispatched three warships to the island, under Captain Geoffery Hornby. Probably no two more unsuited military leaders could have been chosen to deal with the situation. Reports are that both men were stubborn and unwilling to compromise or back down. Both sides refused to relinquish their positions, and reinforcements arrived until the American military presence totaled about 400 men, while the British had five warships and some 2,100 troops anchored just offshore.

For the next twelve years the battle lines were drawn and it looked like hostilities could break out at any minute. Fortunately, cooler heads eventually prevailed and the two nations agreed to an outside arbitrator. In 1872, German's Kaiser Wilhelm I made the final ruling, deciding in favor of the Americans, and the British forces finally withdrew from San Juan Island. The war that wasn't a war was over, it's only casualties some bruised egos, one destroyed garden, and a dead pig.

John Dillinger's Tommy Guns Come Home

Designed for the military, originally used for law enforcement work, stolen by a famous gangster and used in a deadly crime spree, recovered and stored for decades, John Dillinger's Tommy guns have finally made their way back home.

Back in the 1930s, during the hard days of the Great Depression, banks were failing at an alarming rate, wiping out people's life savings in the process, and those who held on did so by foreclosing on farms and factories in record numbers. So it is not surprising that, given the mood of the times, outlaws who preyed on these same banks took on the persona of folk heroes to many otherwise law abiding citizens. It was the Gangster Era, and thugs like Baby Face Nelson, Pretty Boy Floyd, Clyde Barrow, and Bonnie Parker were household names. Though their deeds were too often written in the blood of innocent police officers and honest businessmen, to a great number of out of work, bankrupt, disillusioned Americans, their exploits seemed almost justifiable.

In those lawless days, the name of one cold blooded killer and bank robber stood out from the rest. John Dillinger was Public Enemy Number 1, and the trail of empty bank vaults and dead police officers his gang left in their wake as they blazed their way across the Midwest still stands out in the annals of crime.

Born June 22, 1903 in Indianapolis, Indiana, John Dillinger had been in and out of trouble as a teenager, even serving time in the state reformatory. As he grew older his recklessness and criminal activity increased. He robbed his first bank on June 10, 1933, getting away with $10,600. After a series of bank heists, Dillinger was captured and held in the Allen County Jail in Lima, Ohio, from which members of his outlaw gang freed him in a daring raid on October 12, 1922, killing Sheriff Jesse Sarber in the process.

What followed was another string of bank robberies and bloodshed. The gang robbed the Central National Bank of Greencastle, Indiana of $75,000 less than two weeks later and participated in several other holdups, always one step ahead of the law. On January 15, 1934 Dillinger's gang robbed the First National Bank in East Chicago, Indiana and killed Patrolman William O'Malley in a wild shootout while making their escape. The brave police officer managed to shoot Dillinger several times before he died, but the outlaw's bulletproof vest saved him.

With the heat on, the desperados decided a change of scenery might be healthy and traveled west to Tucson, Arizona. They were staying in a Tucson hotel when the building caught fire. Suspicions were raised when they bribed a couple of firemen to remove several heavy suitcases while the blaze still burned, and soon after a tipster alerted police. John Dillinger and gang members Harry Pierpoint, Russell Clark, and Charles Makley were arrested without a fight.

Dillinger's three henchmen were extradited back to Ohio to stand trial for the murder of Sheriff Sarber, while Dillinger himself was brought back to Indiana to face charges for killing Officer O'Malley. Dillinger was a media darling and posed for photographs with his arresting officers while in custody. Held in the Lake County Jail in Crown Point, Indiana, reporters swarmed around the place hoping for a glimpse of the gangster.

Wary that what was left of the Dillinger gang might attempt to break their leader out of jail a second time, extra police officers were brought in to surround the jail. Indeed, John Dillinger was not planning to overstay his welcome in Crown Point, but he did not need any help in busting out.

On March 3, 1934, wielding what police officers claimed was a smuggled pistol and Dillinger later boasted was a wooden gun he had carved while sitting in his cell, the outlaw overpowered his guards and escaped from the heavily defended jail, taking along a fellow prisoner named Herbert Youngblood. The fleeing prisoners held a guard hostage and drove away in the sheriff's own car, taking along two Thompson submachine guns they had relieved from guards as they made their way outside.

The Thompson submachine gun, affectionately nicknamed the Tommy gun by its many fans, was originally designed for trench warfare during World War I, but full production of the weapons did not start until just before the Armistice was signed. In those days there were no laws restricting private ownership of machine guns, and thousands of the short, heavy firearms were sold to the general public. They were a favorite of ranchers and farmers, who liked them for killing coyotes.

With a high rate of fire, and using powerful .45 ACP ammunition, Tommy guns have seen action in every conflict from World War II to Vietnam, and they are still in use in some parts of the world today. Police departments and gangsters alike quickly realized the deadly efficiency of the Tommy gun, and they were popular on both sides of the law. The Thompson submachine gun is truly an intimidating weapon.

When Dillinger was brought to Crown Point, nearby Porter County loaned its Tommy gun to Lake County to help in guarding the jail. That weapon, along with another owned by Lake County, were the two taken in the jailbreak.

Shortly after making good their escape, Dillinger and Herbert Youngblood split up, and Youngblood was killed a few days later in a shootout with police in Port Huron, Michigan. But nobody knew where John Dillinger was. The outlaw had gone to ground and spent weeks hiding out from the massive manhunt going on for him.

Federal agents caught up with Dillinger and other gang members at the Little Bohemia Lodge in Rheinlander, Wisconsin, on April 22, 1934. A vicious gun battle erupted in which gangster Baby Face Nelson killed Special Agent W. Carter Baum and wounded two others. Three innocent citizens were also caught in the crossfire and wounded, one fatally.

After escaping from Little Bohemia, Dillinger and fellow gang member Homer Van Meter had plastic surgery on their faces in the hope of hiding their identity, then kept a low profile for several weeks while they recuperated. During this lull in their activity, John Dillinger was named Public Enemy Number One on June 22, 1934 and the next day a $10,000 reward was announced for his capture, and an additional $5,000 was offered for information leading to his arrest. In the dark days of the Depression these were huge sums of money and the Feds were sure the rewards would lead to the outlaw's downfall. As if in defiance to the reward on his head, on June 30 John Dillinger led his gang on a raid on a South Bend, Indiana bank, where they stole $30,000.

In the end, it was not reward money, but the hope of avoiding deportation that actually led to the tip that ended Dillinger's crime spree. Anna Sage, a Chicago madam who was a friend of Dillinger's mistress, Polly Hamilton, was about to be sent back to her native Romania. She met with Chicago's top FBI agent, Melvin Purvis and offered to trade Dillinger for immunity from deportation. A trap was laid, and on the evening of July 22, 1934, Sage attended a movie at Chicago's Biograph Theatre with Dillinger and his girlfriend. When they left the theater after the movie, FBI agents moved in for the capture. Instead of going peacefully, the outlaw reached into his jacket for a Colt automatic pistol and was killed in a hail of gunfire. The terror reign of John Dillinger ended in a dirty alley next to the Biograph Theater.

When Dillinger broke out of the Crown Point, Indiana jail he kept the Tommy gun Porter County had loaned to Lake County as his personal weapon and gave the Lake County Tommy gun to one of his gang members, Eddie Green. It was the Porter County gun, serial number 7387, which Dillinger is seen posing with in the famous photograph where he also holds the wooden gun he allegedly used to escape from the jail. Both weapons were used in the five month long crime spree that followed the escape. Eddie Green was killed by the FBI in an ambush while hiding out in St. Paul, Minnesota. Following the shootout that killed Green, the Lake County Tommy gun was sent to FBI headquarters in Washington, D.C. where it remained for 68 years.

The night John Dillinger was killed in Chicago, it is believed Anna Sage's son took the Lake County Tommy gun, ammunition, and a bulletproof vest from the room where the outlaw was staying in their apartment and threw them in Lake Michigan to hide any evidence that could link his family to the gangster. Two days later some boys found the weapon when swimming and notified police. The gun was turned over to the FBI and also taken to Washington, DC, where both guns were put on public display for a time, then locked away in vaults where they sat for decades.

Enter Gordon Herigstad, a firearms historian that specializes in Thompson submachine guns. Doing research on one of his projects in 2001, Herigstad traced the two stolen Thompsons to FBI headquarters in Washington, DC, and helped Lake and Porter Counties recover them. In ceremonies held in 2002, the guns were presented to the current county sheriffs by FBI officials. At long last, John Dillinger's stolen Tommy guns were back home.

Hergistad said that both firearms have tremendous historical value, the Lake County Tommy gun more so than Porter County's gun, because Dillinger used it personally in several of his crimes. It is believed the gun would be worth upwards of a half million dollars to a Thompson collector. But Hergistad hopes neither gun will be sold into a collection, where they will disappear from public sight. He thinks the guns need to be put on display, not as a tribute to John Dillinger and his band of thugs, but in memory of the brave police officers who have been killed while trying to bring men like John Dillinger and his kind to justice.

The Peshtigo Fire

We've all heard the story of the great Chicago Fire, the conflagration that killed as many as 300 citizens and destroyed many of the city's buildings. Ironically, on that very same night an even more terrible holocaust occurred in the small logging town of Peshtigo, 250 miles away in northern Wisconsin. The terrible firestorm that raged through Wisconsin's forests and towns killed at least 1,300 people in and around the booming lumber mill town of Peshtigo, and left a heap of smoldering ashes in its wake. The Peshtigo Fire remains history's greatest recorded loss by fire.

In 1871 Peshtigo was at the very top of a gigantic boom. Timber was king, and Wisconsin's forests were the source of vast supplies of logs, which were floated down the Peshtigo River to the town's lumber mills. Any man looking for work had his choice of jobs in the lumber mills, the world's largest woodworking factory, with the railroad, or with many other employers hard up for help.

Peshtigo's population of 1,750 was swelled by hundreds of lumberjacks, railroad men, and other transient workers. The town's stores, hotels, saloons, and brothels were all doing a booming business, and cash registers were ringing all over town. Outside the town's boundaries, in the farming area known as Sugar Bush, some 300 families added to Peshtigo's economy, supplying fresh produce, milk, and eggs, and purchasing clothing and supplies.

But things were not all well and good. The spring and summer of 1871 were unusually dry and hot. Only two rainfalls had occurred between July and September, and creeks and ponds everywhere were drying up. Water levels in the Peshtigo River had dropped dramatically, and the nearby swamps, once impenetrable, were now dried prairies of peat. Peshtigo's wells were giving out and water was becoming a precious commodity. As the severe drought continued, the dense woods and grasslands of northern Wisconsin were tinder dry. Farmers and townspeople alike knew they were sitting on a powder keg and dreading the spark that could set it off.

Several small fires had broken out around town, but volunteer firemen had quickly extinguished the flames before they could get out of control. As far south as Green Bay, conditions were much the same. For weeks smoke from smoldering peat fires hung in the air, stinging eyes and burning throats. At night the ominous glow of distant wildfires silhouetted the town's buildings and outlying farms.

Sunday morning, October 8, 1871, the sun struggled to shine through the dense smoke. As folks in Peshtigo bustled about getting ready for church, none could have any idea of the horrors that lay ahead in the next few hours. Everyone was nervous as they attended worship services and went home to do their regular chores. There seemed to be a feeling in the air that *this* could be the day.

As the hot afternoon wore on and turned into evening, a sudden wind came in from the southwest, carrying with it a fine white ash that fell on Peshtigo like snowflakes. The wind lifted the smoke just enough to give people a quick glance at the flickering fires moving closer. Just as quickly as it came the wind was gone, leaving behind an eerie dead calm.

In the town's churches and saloons people noticed the sudden calm and increasing heat, and many hurried to their homes to await whatever was coming. Nervous mothers put their children to bed and tried to comfort them in the stifling heat. Meanwhile, concerned fathers kept a wary eye on the distant glow.

Just after 8:30 p.m. the people of Peshtigo were alarmed when a dull roar like that of an approaching tornado, or maybe a distant freight train, grew out of the southwest. The bell on the Catholic church began to ring as the strange noise became louder and the distant glow began drawing nearer.

Suddenly the wind was back again and even stronger than before! Men pulled on their clothes and hurried to the edge of town, ready for another night of firefighting. But this was a fire that no mortal man could battle.

By 10 p.m. the wind was at tornado force, tearing through Peshtigo and shaking the very earth. Flames raced forward at horrific speeds, huge balls of fire shot hundreds of feet into the air before crashing back to earth and exploding, showering everything around them in flames. The firefighters quickly realized that the town could not be spared, and rushed home to try to save their families.

Suddenly the roaring wind tore a burning roof off a building and sailed it over the town, where it shattered in midair, throwing hundreds of burning shards on the buildings below. Panicked townspeople fled from the great wall of fire that descended on the community. Parents grabbed children, husbands held onto their wives, and everyone rushed toward the safety of the river. Many never made it.

The accounts left by survivors of the maelstrom tell of the horrors they experienced. Whole families suddenly burst into flames as they ran away, or fell poisoned by gases carried on the dense smoke. Everywhere one looked there were scenes no horror movie could ever duplicate as friends and neighbors ran past engulfed in flames. Several people with weak hearts collapsed and died in the face of such unspeakable terror. One poor father, realizing his family could not escape and faced horrible deaths in the flames, killed his wife and three children before committing suicide. Another man hung himself rather than face the agony of being burned to death.

Many people were trampled in the mad rush to the river. Husbands carried or drug the lifeless bodies of their wives and children behind them, unwilling to leave them to the flames. Others suffocated or were burned to death as they tried to battle the inferno, hoping to hold it back long enough to allow others to escape. Some 65 people crowded inside a boarding house, hoping its thick walls could shelter them, and died there together when it burst into flames.

Once the fleeing people reached the river, things were just as bad. Unable to swim, some drowned, while others were pushed underwater by the weight of terrified animals and people seeking refuge from the firestorm. Huge vats of animal fat from rendering plants on the river's edge burst into flames, killing many as it turned a stretch of the river into liquid fire. The ground itself became a furnace, and flames leapt 20,000 feet into the air. Many of those who did survive the fire suffered horrible burns.

Things were just as terrible out in the Sugar Bush farming area. The mad flames devoured everything in their path as they rushed forward. Boulders split from the intense heat, and just as in town, people died from poisonous gases carried on the smoke. Animals died in their stalls, or broke free and crushed their owners in stampedes. The few people who survived in the outlying areas managed to do so by finding small creeks with a trace of water, or by laying low in ravines or freshly plowed fields, where they lay in agony as the flames rolled over them. Out of over 300 farms in the Sugar Bush, only eight survived the fire.

Just before dawn the firestorm burned itself out, the wind died, and blackened survivors crawled out of the river and their hiding holes and began stumbling through the smoldering ashes of what had been their town, looking for their families. Soot-covered children poked through the ashes looking for their parents, while mothers sobbed over the bodies of their babies. The only structure still standing was the framework of an unfinished house. The grotesquely twisted bodies of the dead lay everywhere. Some who lived through that terrible night died in the light of day from their injuries, or, their clothing burned off, fell ill from exposure.

As the survivors stumbled about in a trance, one townsman, Big John Mulligan, set off on foot to walk the six miles to the neighboring town of Marinette for help, despite the fact that he himself was badly burned. Before noon, wagon loads of relief supplies and crews of men began arriving in Peshtigo. As the dead were gathered, injured victims of the fire were transported to a Marinette hotel that was turned into a makeshift hospital for treatment. Tents were brought in to shelter the survivors and rescue workers. When word of the fire reached Green Bay, more supplies and rescue workers were rushed to Peshtigo.

The work of gathering the dead went on all day and night. Several hundred victims, burned too badly to be identified, were buried in a mass grave. A marker at the Peshtigo Cemetery stands today to mark the grave.

There is no way to know for sure how many people died in the Peshtigo Fire, since there were many transient workers and loggers in the town for the weekend, and there was no way to account for them all.

Many ironies occurred with the Peshtigo Fire. While many of the people who survived did so by seeking refuge in the river, and creeks, all fish life was destroyed. The heat in one farmer's field was so intense it burned massive stumps right out of the ground, leaving only gaping holes where they had been, while a neighboring field of corn shocks was untouched. Workers sifting through the ashes found the white wooden tabernacle that held the sacred vessels of the Catholic church on the bank of the river, where the priest had carried it, untouched by the fire. Yet everything for yards around it had been destroyed. Iron wagon wheels had melted into lumps, while a bible was not even scorched. The horrific fire that had taken so many lives also spared one. When a thief was found looting the dead, a hasty trial was held and he was sentenced to be hung. But not a rope remained in Peshtigo

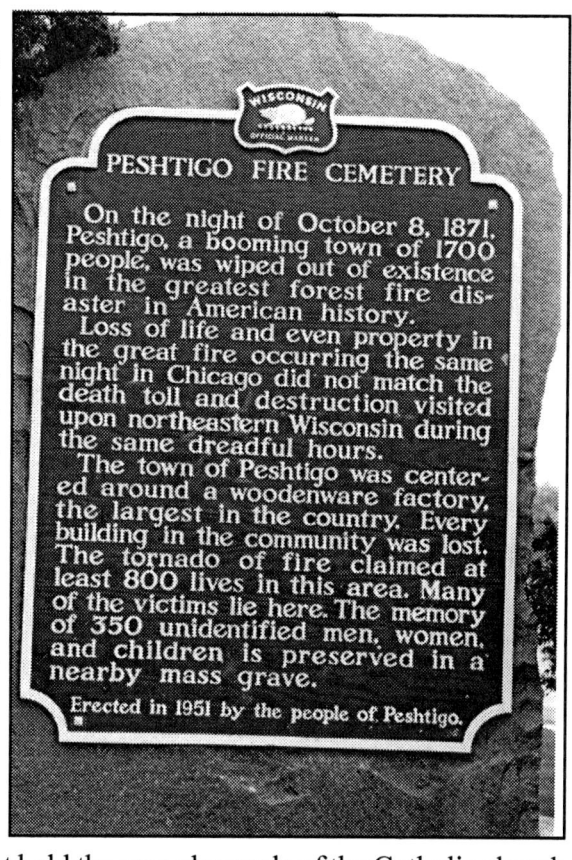

Highway History And Back Road Mystery

to perform the execution, and he was eventually released.

The people of Peshtigo, having survived the fire, began the rebuilding process. Over time the once-thriving economy returned. Years later, as if fate were atoning for the fire, Peshtigo was one of the few towns in America untouched by the Great Depression of the 1930s.

Today Peshtigo is a pleasant, hardworking small city of friendly people, located on US Highway 41. Several small industries provide

Highway History And Back Road Mystery

a healthy economy, and tourism dollars flow in from fishermen, campers, and visitors. The Peshtigo River is popular with anglers looking to hook northern pike in the 15 to 20 pound class, as well as trout, walleye, bass, and salmon. In the winter, snowmobilers and cross country skiers come to explore miles of countryside, and the city has its own campground with electric and water hookups for RVs.

The story of the Peshtigo Fire is told at the Peshtigo Fire museum, located in the center of town. The museum is housed in a building that was the first church built after the fire. Over 17,000 visitors come to tour the museum annually. It is open from 9 a.m. to 4:30 p.m. daily from Memorial Day to October. There is no admission charge, but donations are welcome. The Peshtigo Fire Cemetery, with the mass grave of the fire victims, is located next to the museum.

Highway History And Back Road Mystery

Monument To A Camel Jockey

In a tiny cemetery just off the main drag in Quartzsite, Arizona a monument recognizes one of the strangest experiments ever conducted in the American West, and the man who was instrumental to that experiment.

In the early decades of the 1800s the Army was attempting to chart the vast and wild Arizona Territory to prepare it for settlement. Secretary of War Jefferson Davis, who would later become President of the Confederacy during the Civil War, approved a plan to experiment with using camels as beasts of burden, as they were in other areas of the world.

Two boatloads of the animals were delivered to Texas in February, 1856, then transported to Arizona. With the camels came a Syrian camel driver named Hadji Ali. Since the camels were not trained to understand English, and none of the Army's mule skinners could speak Arabic, Hadji Ali quickly proved his worth. He was a friendly fellow and always eager to please. The solders affectionately changed his name to Hi Jolly.

In 1857 a former Navy officer turned Army man, Lieutenant Edward F. Beale, was responsible for laying out a wagon route through the Arizona desert from Fort Defiance to California, and the camels were attached to Beale's expedition.

Whether the camel experiment would have been successful will never be known – the beasts were too cantankerous to suit Army tastes, and the outbreak of the Civil War drew interest and military resources away from Arizona. Most of the Army went east to fight in the war, and the camels were turned loose in the desert to fend for themselves. For years they roamed in the area around Quartzsite until they finally died off. Hi Jolly never returned to his homeland. He remained in Arizona, where he did some prospecting and lived out his days around Quartszite.

When he died, a pyramid-shaped monument was erected to the camel driver who was a friend to many in the desert. Besides his monument, Hi Jolly was honored in a song by the New Christy Minstrels in the 1960s.

You can visit Hi Jolly's monument in Quartzsite by turning north from the main street, across from the Pilot truck stop. There is a large parking area near the cemetery where you can park while you pay your respects to Arizona's resident camel jockey.

Highway History And Back Road Mystery

More Great Reading From The Gypsy Journal

Meandering Down The Highway: A Year On The Road With Fulltime RVers
Follow a pair of overworked, stressed out baby boomers as they say goodby to the rat race and find a new life as fulltime RVers, and share their experiences during their first year on the road. $20.45 postpaid.

Work Your Way Across The USA: You Can Travel And Make A Living Too!
Presenting the many ways RVers can make a full or part time income to support their traveling lifestyle. $16.45 postpaid.

Gypsy Journal's Guide To Free Campgrounds & Overnight Parking Spots Save hundreds of dollars as you travel with this great listing of over 500 city and county parks, businesses, and public lands where you can camp for free! Many include either full or partial hookup sites. $8.95 postpaid.

RVers Guide To Fairgrounds Camping - Most RVers never realize how many great, money saving camping opportunities fairgrounds have to offer. This guide to over 250 fairgrounds nationwide is a must for every budget conscious RV owner. $7.50 postpaid.

RVers Guide To Modem Friendly Truck Stops - If you travel with a laptop computer, this guide to over 250 truck Stops nationwide where you can access e-mail will make it easy for you to get online. Don't be out of touch just because you're out of town! $6.95 postpaid.

Gypsy Journal's Guide to Public RV Dump Stations - A must-have for every traveling RVer and boon-docker, this new booklet lists nearly 1,000 RV dump stations from coast to coast and in Canada too $7.50 postpaid.

RVers Guide To Casino Parking - Casinos. They're not just for gambling anymore. Many casinos offer RVers free or low cost overnight parking opportunities from coast to coast? We have assembled a list of RV-friendly casinos from across the country where you will find a safe place to park for free or at low cost, enjoy a good meal and an evening's entertainment as well if you need to unwind from a hard day on the road. Order your copy today and start saving money on your next trip! $6.95 postpaid.

Highway History And Back Road Mystery

Special Five In One Deal! - Order all five of our best selling booklets - *Gypsy Journal's Guide To Free Campgrounds & Overnight Parking Spots, Gypsy Journal's Guide to Public RV Dump Stations, RVers Guide To Fairgrounds Camping, RVers Guide To Modem Friendly Truck Stops & RVers Guide To Casino Parking* on one Windows compatible CD or 3.5 inch disk, over $37 value, for just $24.95, postpaid. You save over $13!

Overnight Parking With The VFW - Many VFW Posts welcome traveling veterans who belong to other Posts to pull off the road and spend the night in their parking lots. Some even offer RV hookups! Most Posts do not charge their fellow veterans for this courtesy, and those who do ask only a token fee. We have compiled a list of VFW Posts around the nation that welcome you for a visit. Order your copy today for just $5.50 and reap one of the benefits of your service to your country and your VFW membership.

To order, send check or money order to Gypsy Journal, 1400 Colorado #C-16, Boulder City, Nevada 89005 or order online by logging onto www.PayPal.com and making payment with your credit card to BookOrders@gypsyjournal.net.

CPSIA information can be obtained
at www.ICGtesting.com
Printed in the USA
FFOW02n1647010514
5193FF